HARMONIOUS COLOR SCHEMES

a no-nonsense approach using the Color Wheel

Written and Illustrated by
Elaine Barrette Farmer

Published by White Birch Fine Art, LLC

ISBN: 978-0-9899549-1-4

Dedication

Although it is my students that always thank me for my help in their artistic journey, it is I, who would like to thank all my students, for their untiring support and encouragement in getting me to take my twenty five years of class notes and put them together to create this book.

Contents

Chapter 7: COMPLEMENTARY COLOR SCHEMES

Chapter 8: SPLIT COMPLEMENTARY and ANALOGOUS COMPLEMENTARY COLOR SCHEMES

Chapter 9: ANALOGOUS and MONOCHROMATIC COLOR SCHEMES

Introduction

Overview

This book offers instruction on the use of *The Color Wheel*, a tool that has been in use for many years, developed by The Color Wheel Company. The Color Wheel represents twelve colors: three primary, three secondary and six tertiary colors.

As you learn to use *The Color Wheel* you will see how it serves to simplify color mixing for the artist by using a controlled group of colors to create harmony in artwork.

The front side of the Color Wheel illustrates the color mixes that result when using the primary colors. Black shades and white tints are also illustrated.

The back side of the Color Wheel illustrates a group of stacked geometric shapes representing spatial degrees of separation which, when used, will prove to create harmonious color palettes.

Most students and artists are not inclined to spend precious creative time studying color theory in depth although I do recommend it. I believe that using this tool is the easiest way to simplify color mixing and achieve harmony in your paintings simply and accurately. The Color Wheel is readily available in local art supply stores and online; you may already own one.

The Knowledge you will Gain

You will learn about the twelve basic colors on The Color Wheel, the color bias for each, and their history as well as physical and emotional interpretations. You will also learn how to select color schemes based on the dominant color and choose a color scheme of limited colors. The essence of this approach is to "Simplify, simplify, simplify!"

—Henry David Thoreau ("Where I Lived and What I Lived For" Walden)

The Misnomer

Students come to me frustrated by not being able to get the right pre-mixed tube colors. I began to understand that their frustration came from the lack of knowledge about what colors to choose *before* they start a painting. In addition, they were trying to "color match" all the colors they saw in their reference photos and felt they needed a tube color for each of those colors in the reference.

Too Many Colors

While living in England for three years, I stepped into a local art supply shop to buy some supplies, and I saw that the artist supplies available were fewer than that in our American counterparts. Then, on a painting trip near Siena, Italy, on visiting an art supply shop I again found that there were fewer artist supplies, similar to England. Like so many other products in our country today, we have so many choices, *too* many sometimes. So, I began wondering why we have so many different artists' colors available on the market. That led to paying attention to the ingredients in tube colors which led me to the research for the chapter "What's in your Tube?" An aspect to mixing accurate colors that is seldom addressed.

No Perfect Color, No Magic Potions

There are no perfect tube colors that match the blue of the sky. It does not come from a pre-mixed tube called *Perfect Sky Blue* or some other made-up name by the manufacturers. The question then that begs asking is "Why *are* there so many paint colors to choose from?" The answer is simple. It all comes down to a money maker for manufacturers. The more variety of colors they make, the more colors you think you need, so the more you will buy. Manufacturers feed on the idea that we need to have all those tube colors to create our works of art. In essence, it disables us from actually learning and understanding how to mix color. Color mixing is not difficult when you use a controlled palette using just a few pure colors. Knowing "What's in your Tube" is the second half of the equation. In addition to using pure colors, I will review the use of a wider range of colors that I call convenience colors. High key and neutral colors can also be added. My rule of thumb is to first understand color mixing using a controlled palette of pure colors, then you can add the convenience colors later if you like. The fact remains that with just 12 pure colors in your paint box, you have all the colors you need.

I believe that color mixing should be a little more of a systematic process, not a random one. There are no magic potions for mixing color. The good news, though, is that through practice you will gain knowledge and confidence in your color mixing. The practical knowledge is the easy part; the work comes when you practice it. I often remind my students that there is a reason why art is often referred to as artwork....it does take a bit of work!

My AHA Moment

I attended a workshop by Hongnian Zhang when I learned about the Complementary palette system. The theory based on his book, The Yin/Yang of Painting by Hongnian Zhang and Lois Woolley, was that when you use any Complementary painting scheme (red and green) plus add the warm and cool of each neighboring color, you can successfully mix all the colors need to create any painting and achieve the harmony necessary in doing so. It was this theory that started my exploration of looking at the Itten color wheel more closely and using a number of the different color variations in a Triad and Tetrad spacing of colors. I began experimenting using different limited palettes starting with the simplest of schemes, the Triad color scheme. In doing so, I discovered that I could achieve a great many new colors that worked fine for my paintings, creating the harmony of color that I struggled with for so long. The Triads worked well, so I started experimenting with the Tetrad colors, and found that I had the same degree of success.

My Inspiration

My students are my inspiration. It was my students who encouraged me to write a book on this approach so, based on 3 pages of notes, the book grew. It is based on my many experiences as an artist and teacher. Over the years students admit that previous instructors never taught them *how* to mix color, and when I think back on all my years of instruction and workshops, I think for me it was always expected that I should already know the simple task of mixing color. When a new student comes to me, no matter the artistic level, I start them with the introduction of this simplified approach, and they are amazed when they learn how easy the process is. They quickly have a clearer understanding about color mixing and go on to embrace the simplicity of it in all their works.

Simplified Method for All

This method is suitable for the beginner student as well as the professional artist. It can be applied to any subject or style of art including abstract, expressionism or impressionism and can be applied to all painting mediums including beyond paint such as fiber art and interior decorating. Color harmony is essential to *all* good art no matter the subject, style or medium.

The Work Effect

Whether you are just beginning your art journey or have been struggling to mix color, this systematic approach will help you get on the right track. No more failed piles of color. No more random color selections. The hit or miss mixing process will become a thing of the past.

I have found that most students and artists do not take the time to paint color charts or do the color studies before a painting. For that reason, I offer workshops on this subject where students can allow themselves the time to really study this subject in depth, through exercises and charts. This book will serve you as a reference guidebook and teaching tool for years to come.

Color mixing can take a lifetime of exploration because of the endless possibilities. For that I am grateful. I have been painting for over forty years and still, it is fun and fresh every time I return to my easel.

"Happy are the painters for they shall not be bored" -Winston Churchill.

If you do not already own a Color Wheel, you may want to have one to follow along. If you do, dust it off and let's get going!

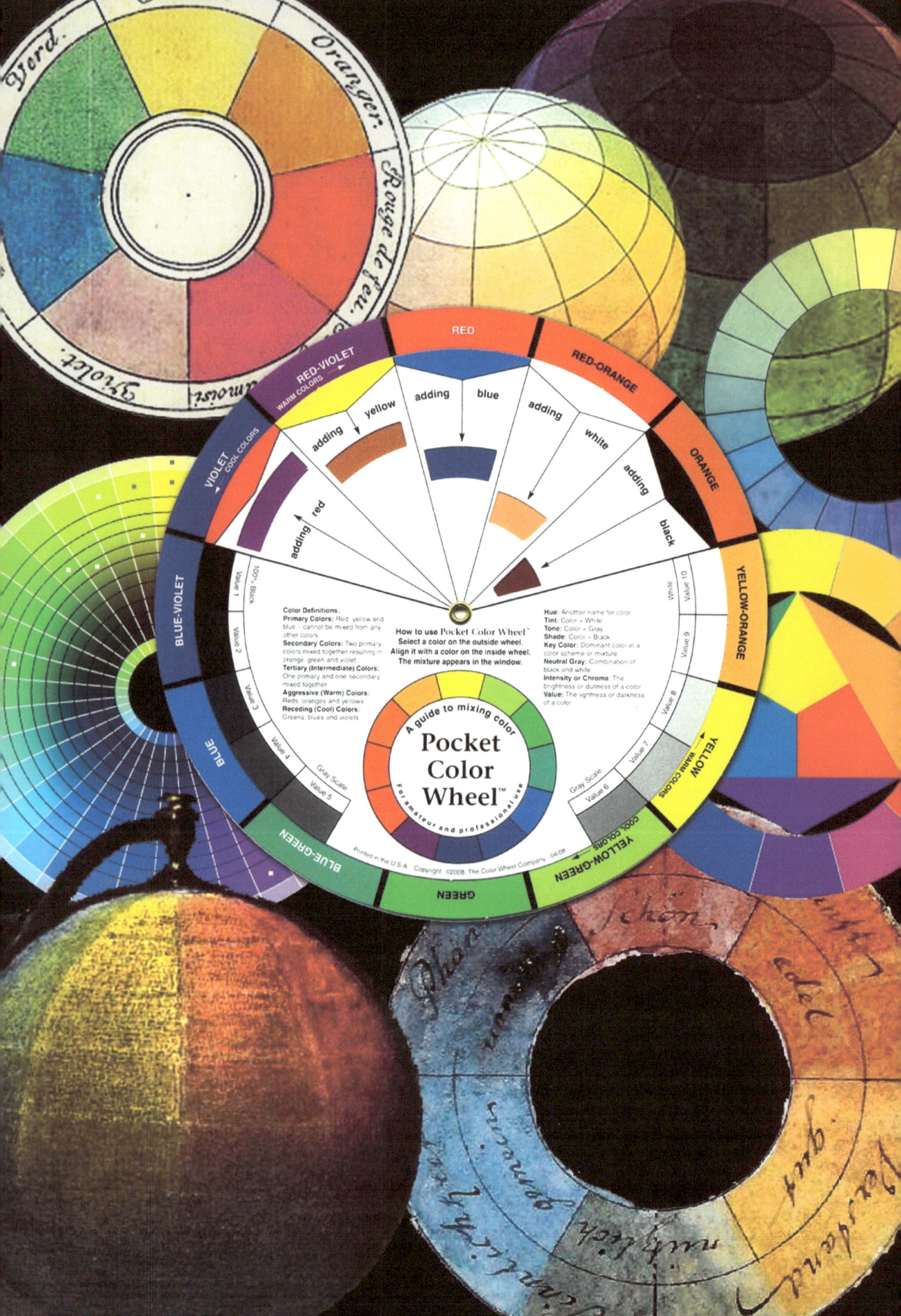

Chapter 1

COLOR WHEEL INTRODUCTION

History of the Color Wheel and its Theory Contributors

The "Everybody is Right" Theory

As you look to expand your knowledge of color mixing you may have found yourself confronted with a number of books on the subject. Choices range from books on the science of color and the spectrum of light as it relates to wavelengths and frequencies, to the new primaries interpreted as Cyan, Magenta, Yellow and Black commonly known as CMYK for the print industry. For the artist, the *Munsell Color Theory* addresses the value, chroma and hue in a three-dimensional view, a more complex system than Newton's original six colors. The list of contributors goes on. For centuries, the theory of mixing color pigment has been argued and re-invented. The debate will continue to remain an important topic of discussion for some time to come as each new school of artists looks to add their own stamp of approval to what is the standard to Color Theory.

Although there are scientific causes for light and color, I have chosen not to include this information. Instead, I would like to offer you a brief selection of major contributors in the history of color theory. It shows the similarities of thought and the different interpretations used through the years; some through science and others through collaboration. All the theories are different but correct. It is what I call the "Everybody is right!" theory.

Isaac Newton (1642-1727) Experiments with light helped Isaac Newton invent the

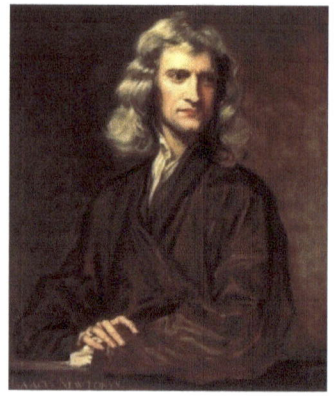

first color wheel in 1666, where he passed a beam of sunlight through a prism, splitting white sunlight into red, orange, yellow, green, cyan, and blue beams. He was then able to show the natural sequence of color by joining the two ends of the color spectrum together.

A common list includes all those colors that can be produced only by visible light of a single wavelength, essentially *pure spectral* or *monochromatic* colors.

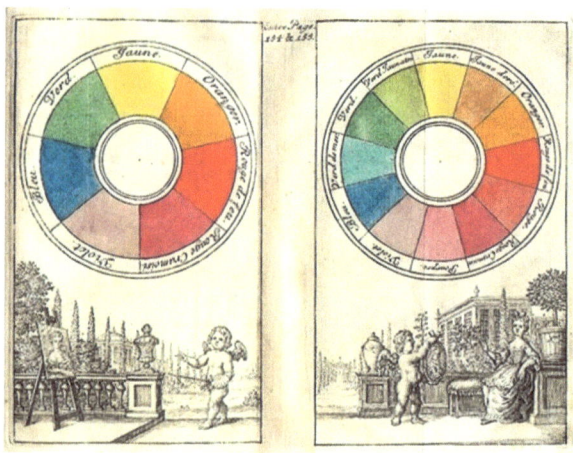

In Newton's color wheel he identified the familiar colors of the rainbow as six main bands of color known as red, orange, yellow, green, blue, and violet. To this list Newton's concept included a seventh color, indigo, between blue and violet.

A century later **Johann Wolfgang von Goethe (1749-1832)** a German writer and

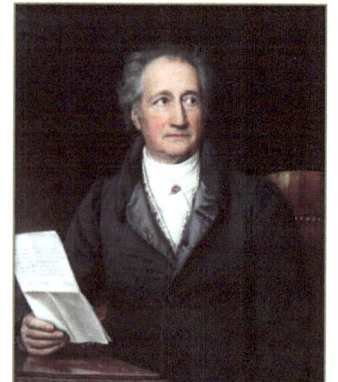

scientist, began studying the psychological effect of colors. He noted that blue evoked quiet moods and red evoked cheerfulness.

Goethe created a color wheel showing the psychological effect of each color. He divided all the colors into two groups – the plus side (from red through orange to yellow) and the minus side (from green through violet to blue). Colors of the plus side produce excitement and cheerfulness. Colors of the minus side are associated with weakness and unsettled feelings.

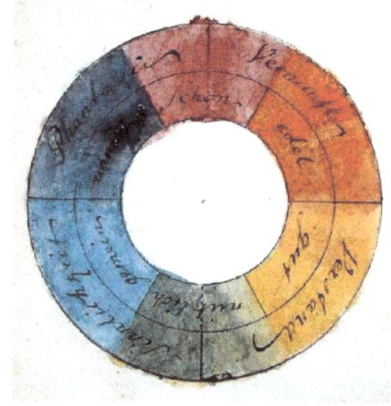

Philipp Runge (1777-1820) was a romantic German painter and draughtsman. He

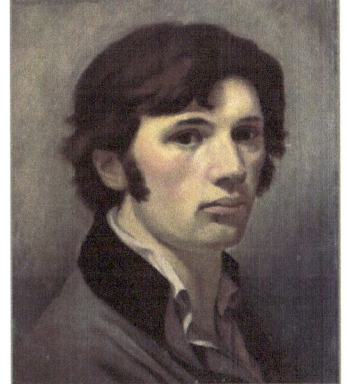

made a late start to his career and died young, nonetheless he is considered among the best German Romantic painters. In 1803, on a visit to Weimar Germany, Runge unexpectedly met Johann Wolfgang von Goethe and the two formed a friendship based on their common interests in color and art.

Runge was responsible for diagramming the color wheel in a three-

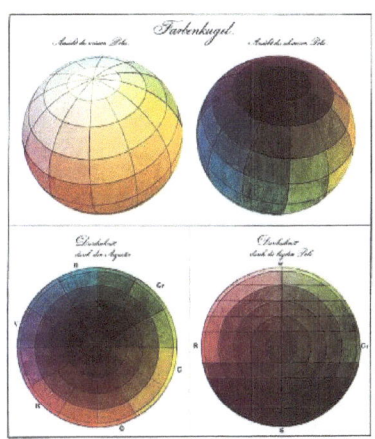

dimensional format. His goal was to establish the complete world of colors resulting from mixture of the three primary colors, among themselves and together with white and black.

He arrived at the concept of the color sphere sometime in 1807, as written in his letter to Goethe of Nov. 21 of that year, by expanding the hue circle into a sphere, with white and black forming the two opposing poles. In the same lengthy letter, Runge discussed in some detail his views on color order and included a sketch of a mixture circle, with the three primary colors forming an equilateral triangle and together with their pair-wise mixtures, a hexagon. Runge's premature death limited the impact of this work. Goethe, who had read the manuscript before publication, mentioned it in his book "Farbenlehre" written in 1810 "successfully concluding this kind of effort".

Albert Munsell (1858-1918) was born in Boston, Massachusetts, attended and served

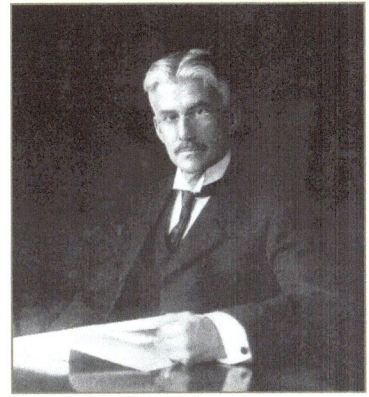

on the faculty of Massachusetts College of Art, and died in nearby Brookline. He was an American painter, teacher of art, and founded the Munsell Color Company in 1917. As a painter, he was noted for seascapes and portraits.

Munsell is famous for inventing the Munsell Color System, an early attempt at creating an exact system for numerically describing colors based on a spherical color order system using Philipp Otto Runge's original concept of the color sphere. He wrote three books about it: A Color Notation (1905), Atlas of The Munsell Color System (1915) and one published posthumously, A Grammar of Color: Arrangements of Strathmore Paper in a Variety of Printed Color Combinations According to The Munsell Color System (1921). The Munsell Color System has gained international acclaim and has served as the foundation for many other color order systems.

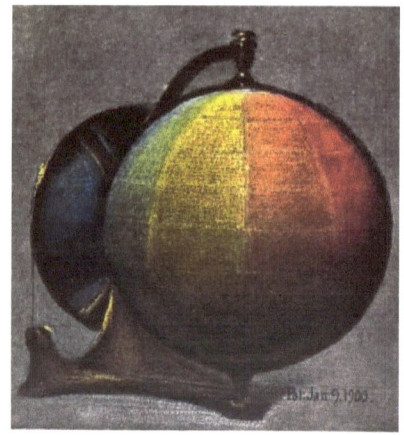

A BALANCED COLOR SPHERE

At the turn of the 20th century, one of the most widely used forms of color theory was

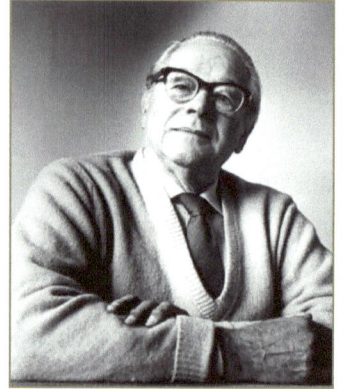

developed by **Johannes Itten (1888-1967)** a Swiss color and art theorist who taught at the School of Applied Arts in Weimar, Germany.

Itten developed 'color chords' and modified the color wheel. Ittens' color wheel is based on red, yellow, and blue colors as the primary colors, orange, green and violet

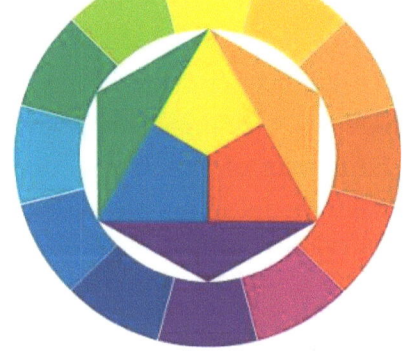

as the secondary colors and six tertiary colors for a total of twelve basic hues. He published his ideas on color theory in his book *The Art of Color,* first published in 1961 and is still in publication today. It is Ittens' theory that The Color Wheel Company bases its twelve step Color Wheel after.

We owe much to each of these contributors and to others along the way for their studies in this subject. Their efforts, either through their scientific study (Newton and Goethe) or their writings (Runge, Munsell and Itten), have educated and inspired artists throughout the ages. They are all connected in their individual efforts by a common thread that I call the "Everybody is Right" Theory.

What is Color Theory?

I often refer to painting like playing an instrument. Musical notes help you to play music, much like knowing how to mix basic colors will help with painting. Art and music share common words like harmony, contrast, accent notes and lines. With twelve colors, it is easier to create a work of art based on knowledge and using a systematic approach, not a hit or miss one.

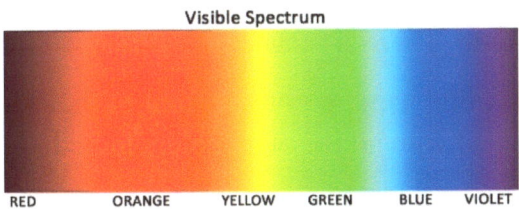

Color Theory is a set of principles derived from the spectrum to create harmonious color combinations. The spectrum does not, however, have all the colors that the human eyes and brain can distinguish. Unsaturated colors such as pink or purple variations such as magenta are absent, for example, because they can only be made by a mix of multiple colors. The color spectrum which is normally seen in a straight band was wrapped into a circle known as the color wheel.

The Front Side of the Twelve Step Color Wheel

The Color Wheel is a visual representation of color theory. Colors are arranged in a circle and for continuity in this book placement of RED is used at the top of the Color Wheel in most illustrations. This represents the beginning of the color spectrum as seen in a prism or rainbow.

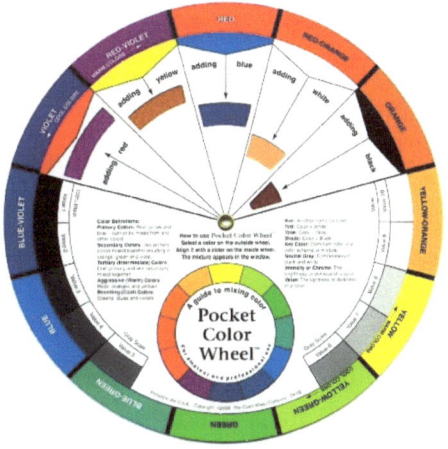

The colors on The Color Wheel are printed with inks so be mindful that these colors will have a different bias than with tube colors.

The primary colors are positioned in equal distance from one another and are **RED, YELLOW** and **BLUE**.

The secondary colors are connected by a bridge of the tertiary colors and are **ORANGE, GREEN** and **VIOLET**.

Tertiary colors are positioned between the primary and secondary colors and therefore have both color titles and are **RED-ORANGE, YELLOW-ORANGE, YELLOW-GREEN, BLUE-GREEN, BLUE-VIOLET** and **RED-VIOLET**.

There are 6 warm colors and 6 cool colors but within each color group, each color group will have a warm and cool bias of itself. Example: RED is a warm color but RED-ORANGE is the warm bias of RED and RED-VIOLET is the cool bias.

The twelve printed colors shown on the Color Wheel are just guidelines, not absolute colors for each color group. There are many bias variations for each group.

The colors shown in the little windows on the front of the Color Wheel represent the three primary colors mixed with all the other colors including black and white.

The Gray Scale values are helpful to name the values of each color.

Note: Throughout this book, whenever you see the color words printed in all capitalized letters, these color names refer to the general color names from the Color Wheel and should be thought as a generalized color group.

The Back Side of the Color Wheel

Let's examine the back of the Color Wheel. If you own a Color Wheel, you have probably seen the little diagram on the back but, like so many, do not understand what it is for. The stacked geometric shapes are spatial degrees of separation which, when used to create harmonious color palettes, serve as a valuable tool.

Starting with the top shape, the first is the isosceles triangle standing for the Split Complementary color scheme. The second is an equilateral triangle, standing for the Triad color scheme. The next two shapes, the rectangle, and the square, both stand for a Tetrad color scheme. By selecting the colors at each corner of any designated scheme, these combinations are designed to work together to form a harmonious Color Palette for the artist.

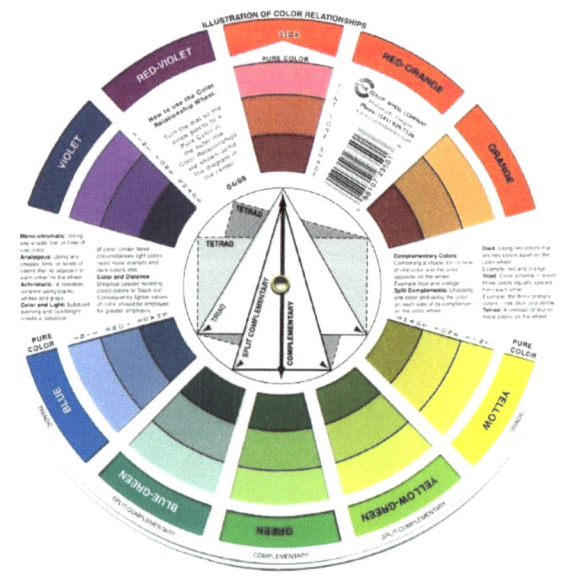

I like to think of it as a "Dial-a-Color Scheme". It is that easy!

Tinting with White

White is most often used to tint or lighten a color, but this can cool a color. To keep the integrity of a color, add a small amount of the color nearest the one you want to lighten in addition to white. This often gives a better result in tinting. Example: if you were painting a red rose, use some yellow and white for a highlight. The White you choose may be opaque or transparent depending on the need. White is a pigment used in most paintings so assume that when a light color is present and mixed with pure pigments in any of the examples, White is used in the mix.

Tone or Shade with Black

It is helpful to use the Gray Value Scale on the front side of the Color Wheel to name a color's value. Both the front and back of the Color Wheel illustrate the use of gray to tone a color and black to shade a color. It is my philosophy that instead of using gray or black, use a Complementary color to shade or tone a color. A Complementary color will neutralize a color, keeping the chromatic value in place. Black will be addressed in the tube pigment section of this book only as a matter of reference.

One more Note before you begin

For the continuity of this book, the color cards, charts, and painting examples are represented in oil color, but the approach described in this book may be applied to all mediums.

Please consider too as you read this book, that the Color Wheel itself is just an interpretation of the generalized color groups, i.e., the BLUE-GREEN on The Color Wheel is often more of a turquoise or aqua color. I prefer to use a darker color such as Phthalo Blue, to represent BLUE-GREEN. You can always lighten a dark color; you cannot darken a lighter version without losing its original intensity.

The color bias in this book may also differ in the print. I have proofed the copy as close as possible but found there to still be variations so please keep this in mind as you read this book. Do not take the colors so literal but interpret them as a generalized version of that color or color group.

Chapter 2

THE TWELVE BASIC COLOR GROUPS

This section is broken up into three main color groups: Primary, Secondary and Tertiary. For each color group the bias is identified as shown through illustrations. A brief History offers interesting insight into their origins. Physical and Emotional Interpretations are included to show how, in art, color can affect the emotion in your paintings.

Color Bias

Color bias is when a color leans toward one of the other primary colors. An example would be a RED with a bias toward yellow might look like Cadmium Red Light. A RED with a bias toward blue may look like Cadmium Red Deep. By learning these differences, it will help you to choose the correct colors.

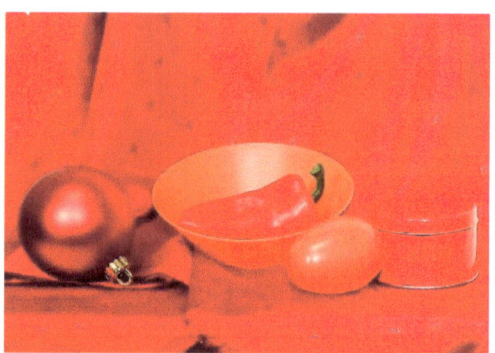

When mixing a secondary color, orange, green or violet, you will use two primary colors with the strongest bias to the color you intend to mix. The illustrations on the following pages will offer a color bias for each.

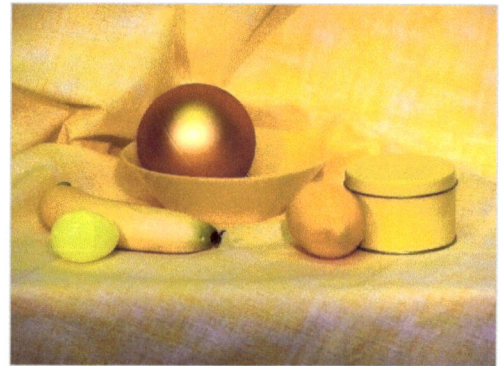

Some color schemes may require a thoughtful adjustment of color using a specific bias but then in some cases it may not affect the color you are mixing as much. Adjust your tube colors in your color scheme with each painting you do. The bias of each color will decide the outcome of the new color.

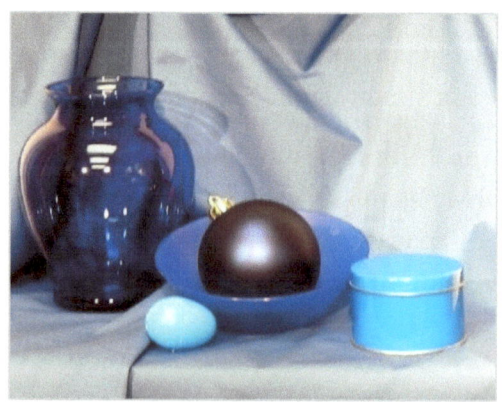

8

PRIMARY COLORS

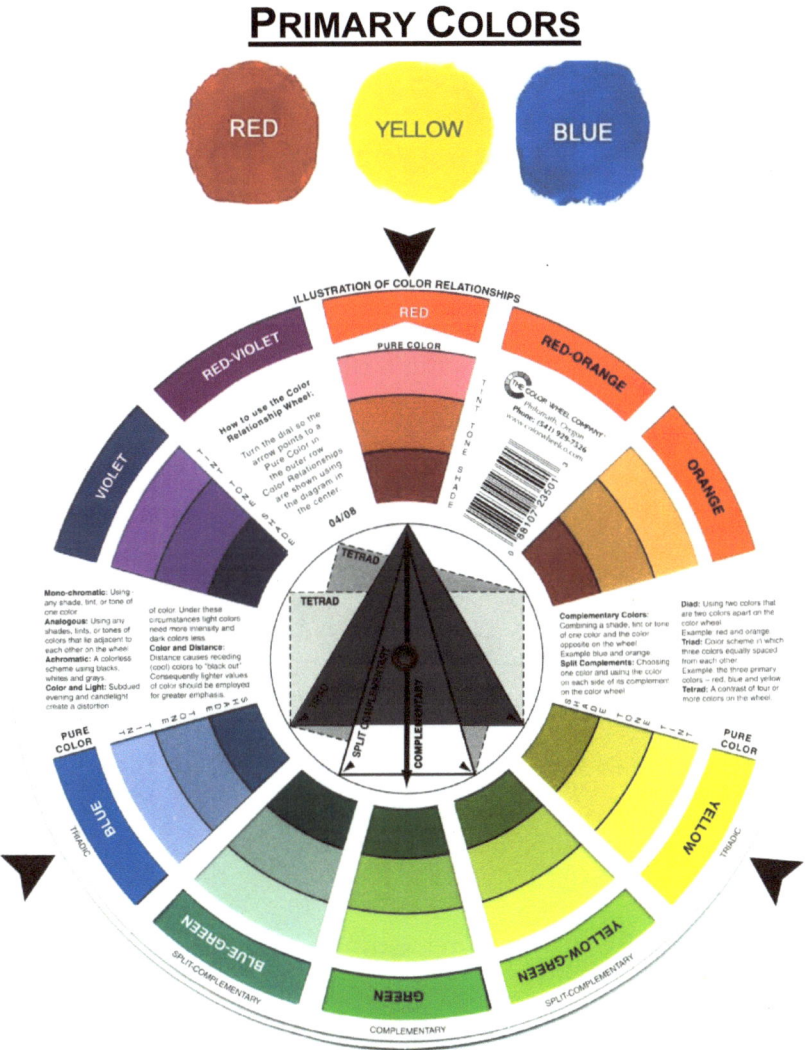

A primary color cannot be mixed using any other colors. These colors are **RED, YELLOW,** and **BLUE**. From these primaries, all other colors can be mixed. The *bias* of these colors is the subject of this section.

It is difficult to say a RED, YELLOW or BLUE are absolute primaries when the bias of each can vary greatly from tube color to tube color.

For the sake of trying to gain clarity of color bias, I suggest the use of Cadmium Red Medium PR108, Hansa Lemon PY3 and Cobalt Blue PB28 as a close resemblance to a primary tube color. This is not to say you may have your own idea of what a primary color stands for, and you may choose a different group of tube colors to use as your primary colors. This is ok. There is no hard and fast rule here.

RED

a warm Primary Color—its Complementary color is GREEN

Cadmium Red PR108 is the color traditionally used for this group. This illustration compares the bias of two different Cadmium Reds made from the same pigment PR108. Cadmium Red Medium (left) is warmer with a yellow bias. Cadmium Red Deep (right) has a cool or blue bias. If you want to mix a clear ORANGE, you may need to choose a Red with a yellow bias like Cadmium Red Light. To mix a clearer Violet, you may need to choose a Red with a Blue bias (Cadmium Red Deep).

Cadmium Red PR108

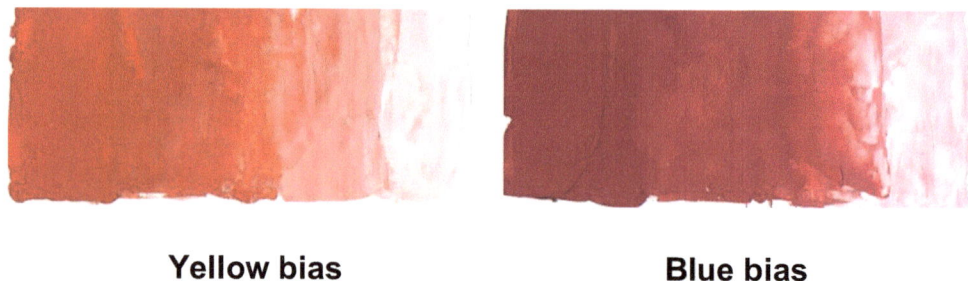

| **Yellow bias** | **Blue bias** |

RED tube color names with index numbers are Cadmium Red PR108, Perylene Red PR149 and Pyrrole Red PR254.

Names associated with RED are Carmine, Crimson, Dark Red, Fire Engine, Rose, and Scarlet.

History

Red pigments have been produced from the earliest days known to man. The first reds found in Late Stone Age where they were scraping and grinding ochre, a red colored clay, iron oxide, probably with the intention of using it to color their bodies.

As early as the eighth century BC a red dye was made by drying and then crushing the bodies of a tiny scale female insect called Kermes vermilion found in Kermes oak trees near the Mediterranean. These dyes were exported as they reached great status and value in Europe and the Middle East. The early inhabitants of Central and South America (800-100 BC), had their own vivid crimson dye, made with the Cochineal insect, of the same family as the Kermes vermilion. Pigments produced from the cochineal insect gave the Catholic cardinals their vibrant robes and the English

"Redcoats" their distinctive uniforms. The true source of the pigment, an insect, was kept secret until the 18th century, when biologists discovered the source.

Cadmiums were discovered in 1817 by Friedrich Strohmeyer but production was delayed until about 1840 due to the scarcity of cadmium metal. It was not widely available as a commercial product until 1919. Cadmium gets its name from the Latin word *cadmia*, meaning *zinc ore calamine*, and the Greek word *kadmeia*, meaning *Cadmean earth*, first found near Thebes.

Physical and Emotional Interpretations

Red brings to mind all things intense and passionate and exciting like burning passion, desire, love, lust and sex. This color may stir up erotic feelings ("Lady in Red", red lips and nails). Put some red in your life when you want more energy. We *feel* in red when engaged in high physical activity or sports, our heart rate increases. RED is Tuesday's color.

The negative traits are aggression, rage, power, violence, and war. Bravery, courage, and strength are types of valor. Red is used on signs of danger and hazard (traffic lights and high voltage signs).

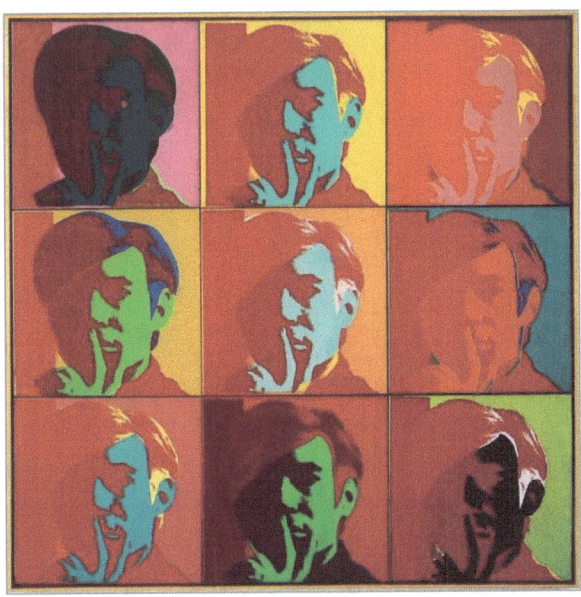

Self Portrait by Andy Warhol
Illustration of a dominant Red painting.

YELLOW

a warm Primary Color—its Complementary color is VIOLET

Hansa PY3 or Cadmium Lemon PY35 is typically used as the color pigment for this group. The example here compares the two different pigments, Hansa PY3 and Cadmium Lemon PY35. They show slight color bias which might be important when making a clear orange. For instance, to produce a bright true ORANGE color, the slightly warmer, red bias yellow, (Cadmium Lemon), would be used to achieve this. When mixing a Green either yellow would produce a green hue so the bias may not be as important.

Hansa PY3 (left) or Cadmium Lemon PY35 (right)

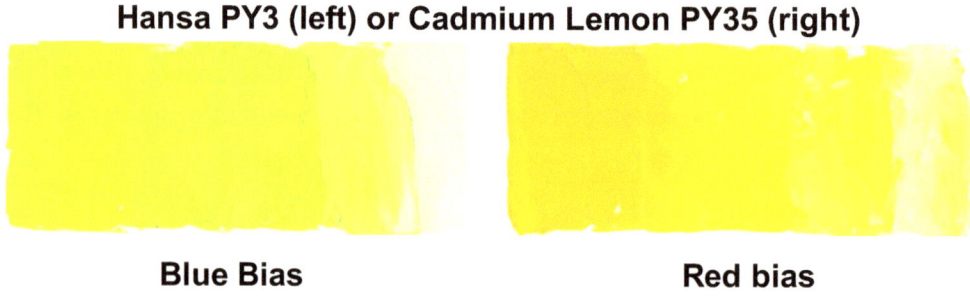

Blue Bias   **Red bias**

YELLOW tube color names with index numbers are Arylide Yellow 5GX PY74, Benzimidazolone Yellow PY175, Cadmium Lemon PY35, and Hansa PY3.

Names associated with YELLOW include Azo, Arylide, Bismuth, Cadmium Yellow Light, Chrome, Hansa, Lemon, Monoazo or Primary Yellow.

History

In some of Vincent van Gogh's paintings, the yellow he used has dulled to coffee-brown, and in about 10 of them, the discoloration is serious, said Koen Janssens, an analytical chemist at Antwerp University in Belgium who co-authored a study to determine the cause of the dulled van Gogh's paintings. The root of the problem is the yellow lead chromate paint he used. This pigment was far brighter and more vibrant than earlier yellows. It was used by artists in the earlier part of the 19th century but has been largely replaced by other more permanent yellow pigments.

The first recorded use of *lemon* as a color name in English was in 1598. Lemon or lemon yellow is the color named after the fruit, for the color of the outer skin of a lemon.

Physical and Emotional Interpretations

Clean light yellow clears the mind, making it active and alert. Yellow is full of creative and intellectual energy. Yellow is naturally associated with the sun, giving and sustaining our energy. Like the energy of a bright sunny summer day, yellow brings clarity and awareness and is associated with joy, hope, and happiness. Yellow produces a warming effect, arouses cheerfulness, stimulates mental activity, and generates muscle energy. People of optimism, wisdom and high intellect favor yellow. Yellow daffodils are a symbol of unrequited love. Yellow is often associated with food. Bright, pure yellow is an attention getter, which is the reason taxicabs are painted this color. In heraldry, yellow says honor and loyalty but in later years the meaning of yellow was connected with cowardice.

The negative traits are betrayal, deceit, dishonesty, and jealousy. It can stand for hazard (in street signs). When overused, yellow may have a disturbing effect; it is known that babies cry more in yellow rooms. Yellow is seen before other colors when placed against black; this combination is often used to issue a warning. Men usually perceive yellow as a very lighthearted, 'childish' color, so it is not recommended to use yellow when selling prestigious, expensive products to men; nobody will buy a yellow business suit or a yellow Mercedes.

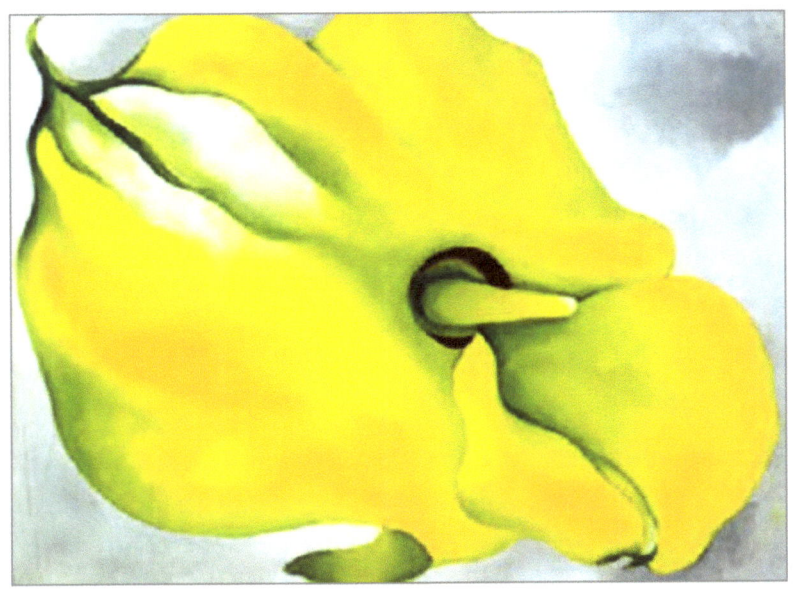

Yellow Calla by Georgia O'Keeffe
Illustration of a dominant Yellow painting.

BLUE

a cool Primary Color—its Complementary color is ORANGE

Cobalt Blue PB28 is the typical color pigment for this group. This BLUE comparison is made from the same pigment Cobalt Blue PB28 but two different manufacturers. The difference is very slight but may be important if you need to make a clear Green in your painting. Using a warmer or cooler Cobalt Blue will produce different colored Greens. If you want to produce a clear Violet, you will want to use a Cobalt Blue with a Red bias.

Cobalt Blue PB28

Yellow bias   **Red bias**

BLUE tube color names with index numbers are Cobalt Blue PB28 and Cobalt Zinc Silicate Blue PB74.

Names associated with BLUE are Delft, Persian, Primary, Royal and True blue.

History

The very costly and extremely stable pigment of pure blue, Cobalt blue, was discovered by Thénard in 1802. It is now the most important of the cobalt pigments. Although smalt, a pigment made from cobalt blue glass, has been known at least since the Middle Ages, the cobalt blue established in the nineteenth century was greatly improved on.

Vincent van Gogh declared to his brother Teo, "Cobalt (blue) is a divine color and there is nothing so beautiful for putting atmosphere around things".

Many artistic contributions have been made referencing clear days with blue skies as part of the happiness or as a symbolism of the happiness the artist felt, such as Tony Bennett's "Put on a Happy Face". If this were untrue there would obviously be more complaints about days with clear blue skies. In the English language Blue is used as a style of Music as in "Singing the Blues".

Physical and Emotional Interpretations

A pure blue is the color of inspiration, sincerity, and spirituality. Blue is the color of the sky, twilight, and the ocean. Blue gives a feeling of distance standing for a heavenly gesture. Artists use it to show perspective in paintings. It is often described as calming, peaceful, serene, and tranquil. Blue is a color standing for loyalty and order. In business or relationships, it is a sign of commitment, confidence, dependability, and trustworthiness. Blue is often the color chosen by conservative people. Wear blue sapphire and blue topaz gemstones to feel calm. Blue is Wednesday's color.

Dark blue stands for knowledge, power, integrity, and seriousness. It holds a cool vibration that is helpful to communication. It is considered a masculine color and the preferred color of men. Blue Monday suggests a dreary depressed day. "Blue Blood" means belonging to or constituting the characteristic of aristocrats especially as derived from feudal times; "of noble birth".

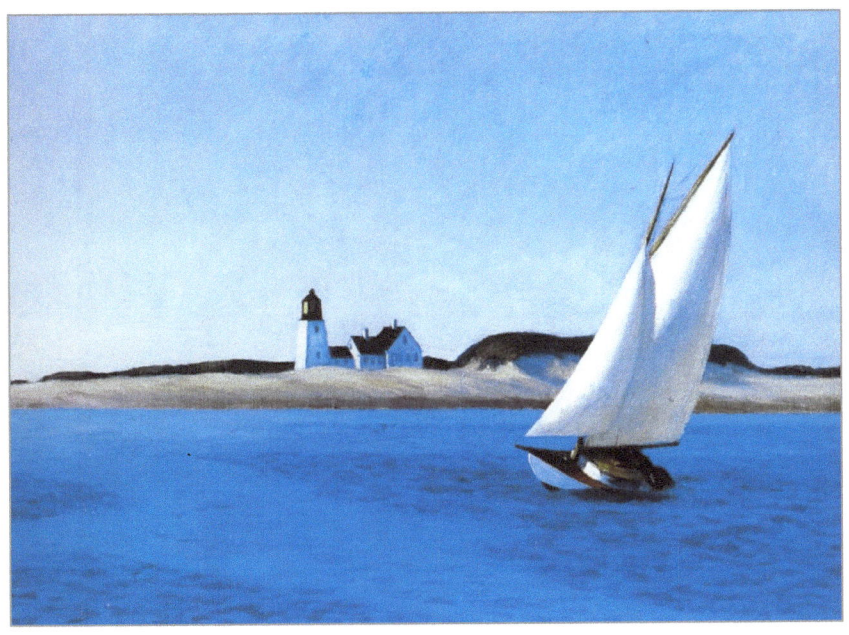

The Long Leg by Edward Hopper
Illustration of a dominant Blue painting.

SECONDARY COLORS

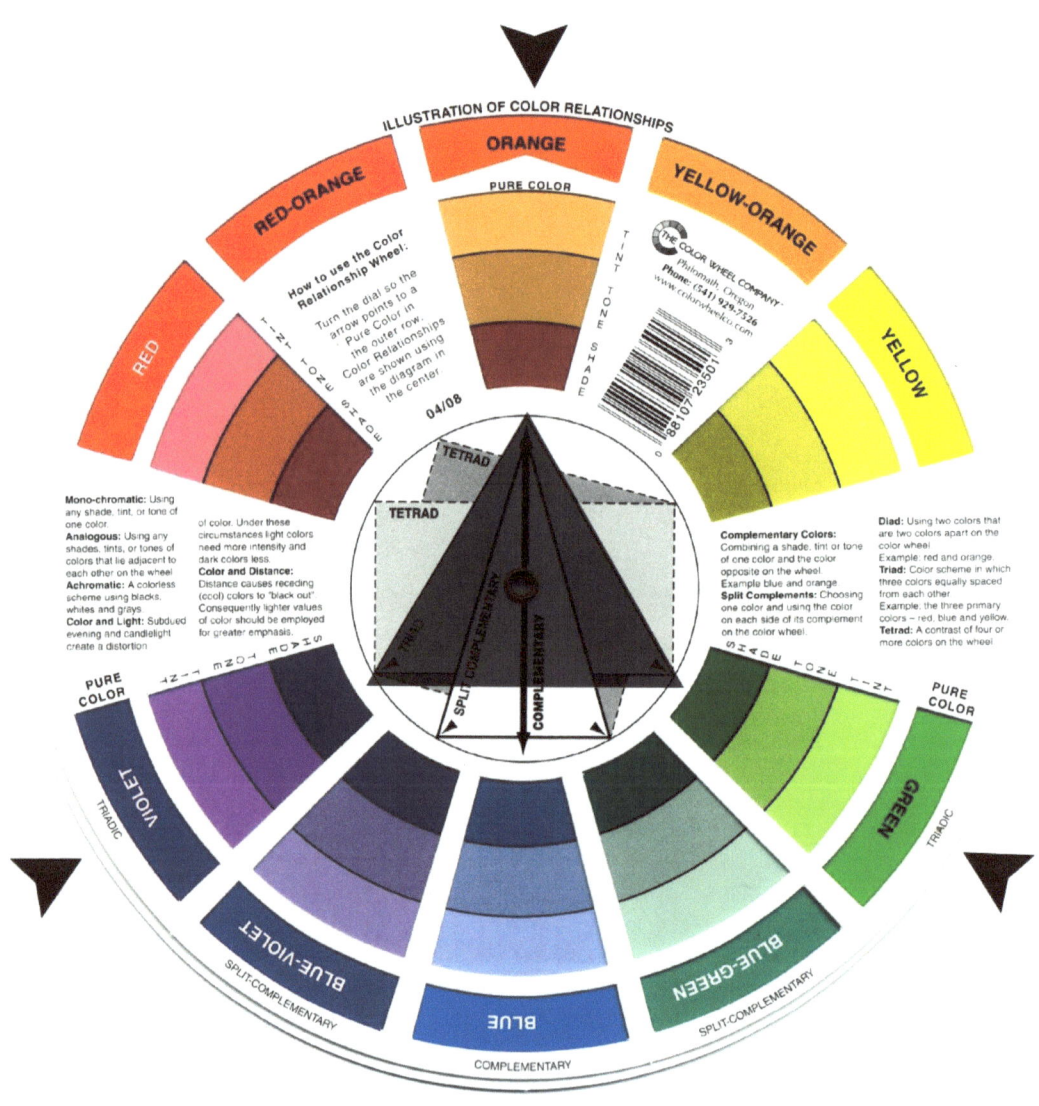

ILLUSTRATION OF COLOR RELATIONSHIPS

ORANGE

RED-ORANGE

YELLOW-ORANGE

PURE COLOR

RED

YELLOW

TINT TONE SHADE

THE COLOR WHEEL COMPANY
Philomath, Oregon
Phone: (541) 929-7526
www.colorwheelco.com

04/08

TETRAD

TETRAD

Mono-chromatic: Using any shade, tint, or tone of one color.
Analogous: Using any shades, tints, or tones of colors that lie adjacent to each other on the wheel.
Achromatic: A colorless scheme using blacks, whites and grays.
Color and Light: Subdued evening and candlelight create a distortion

of color. Under these circumstances light colors need more intensity and dark colors less.
Color and Distance:
Distance causes receding (cool) colors to 'black out'. Consequently lighter values of color should be employed for greater emphasis.

Complementary Colors:
Combining a shade, tint or tone of one color and the color opposite on the wheel.
Example blue and orange.
Split Complements: Choosing one color and using the color on each side of its complement on the color wheel.

Diad: Using two colors that are two colors apart on the color wheel.
Example: red and orange.
Triad: Color scheme in which three colors equally spaced from each other.
Example: the three primary colors – red, blue and yellow.
Tetrad: A contrast of four or more colors on the wheel.

SPLIT COMPLEMENTARY

COMPLEMENTARY

TRIAD

PURE COLOR

VIOLET

GREEN

PURE COLOR

SHADE TONE TINT

TRIADIC

TRIADIC

BLUE-VIOLET

BLUE-GREEN

SPLIT-COMPLEMENTARY

BLUE

SPLIT-COMPLEMENTARY

COMPLEMENTARY

16

SECONDARY COLORS

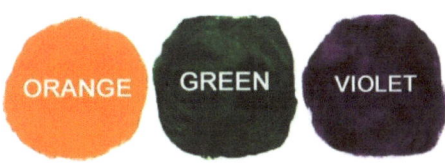

Secondary Colors are colors that are mixed using the primary colors.

Mixing secondary colors is not only about the proportions in which you mix two primary colors, but you must also know what the bias is in each of the contributing colors.

When mixing secondary colors, be sure each contributing tube color has only one pure color pigment, i.e., if you were making a bright green, you might choose Phthalo Blue PB15 and Hansa or Lemon Yellow PY3 (see illustrations under GREEN section).

Pure tube color pigments for the secondary colors; ORANGE, GREEN and VIOLET, can offer more brilliant versions than from mixes. It will be your decision as to which colors work best for a particular painting.

Using the secondary colors in a Triad color scheme may be one of the most challenging. You need to carefully select each color by asking yourself what the bias of each color needs to be. By creating multiple charts using differing biases you will be able to decide which color is best for the work you wish to produce.

ORANGE

a warm Secondary Color—its Complementary color is BLUE

Cadmium Orange PO20 is the typical color pigment for this group. When using ORANGE in a color scheme, the color bias you choose can be important especially if your scheme does not include a yellow. The bias of Orange may vary from a yellow bias to a red bias. Manufacturers' bias is also subjective in how they choose to lean the bias. These two examples illustrate Cadmium Orange produced by two different manufacturers.

Cadmium Orange PO20

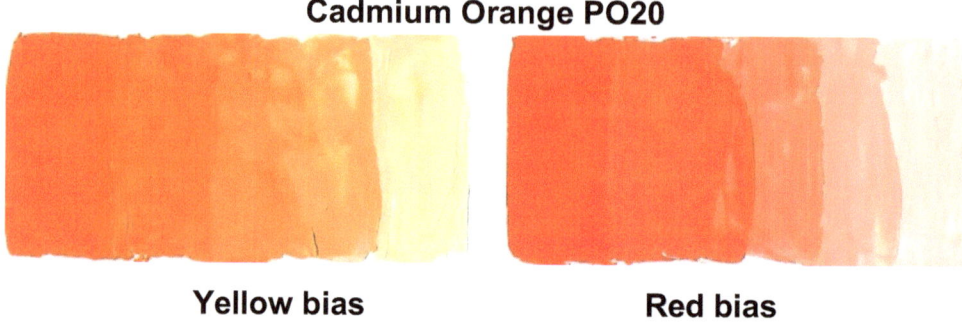

Yellow bias   **Red bias**

ORANGE tube color names with index numbers are Cadmium Orange PO20, Perinone Orange PO43, Pyrazoloquinazolone Orange PO67 and Pyrrol Orange PO73.

Color names associated with ORANGE are Apricot, Gamboge, Orange, Peach, Saffron and Tangerine.

History

Cadmium Orange was the first true orange and was made by mixing Cadmium Yellow with Cadmium Red. Cadmium pigments have been partially replaced by Azo compounds, which are similar in lightfastness to the cadmium colors but cheaper and non-toxic.

The color is named after the orange fruit, introduced to Europe via the Sanskrit word naranja. Before this was introduced to the English-speaking world, the color was referred to (in Old English) as geoluhread, which translates into Modern English as yellow-red.

Orange became an important color for all the impressionist painters. They all had studied recent books on color theory, and they knew that orange placed next to azure blue made both colors much brighter. Auguste Renoir painted boats with stripes of chrome orange paint straight from the tube. Paul Cezanne did not use orange pigment, but created his own oranges with touches of yellow, red, and ochre against a blue background. Toulouse Lautrec often used oranges in the skirts of dancers and gowns of Parisiennes in the cafes and clubs he portrayed. For him it was the color of festivity and amusement.

Orange, or more specifically deep saffron, is the most sacred color of Hinduism. Clothing in this color has been regularly worn in different parts of the world, particularly in religious ceremonies, in India. Orange is the national color of the Netherlands.

Physical and Emotional Interpretations

To the human eye, orange is a hot color (warmest color on the Color Wheel) and gives the sensation of heat. Orange can enhance the appetite and increase the craving for food. It also stimulates success, enthusiasm, creativity, and mental activity. People who like the color orange are usually thoughtful and sincere. Lady luck's color is orange. If a change of any kind is needed in life, burn an orange candle for clarity. It is one of the healing colors. Fun and flamboyant orange radiates warmth and cheerful energy. In heraldry, orange is symbolic of strength and endurance. While red is associated with fiery heat, orange is associated with the benign warmth of the sun. A dynamic color to be sure, orange offers a more thoughtful control, confidence, and trust than explosive red. Curiosity is a driving characteristic of orange, and with it comes exploration of new things.

Orange is a power color. There is usually strong positive or negative association to orange and true orange generally elicits a stronger "love it" or "hate it" response than other colors. It can create feelings of depression & tension. **Dark orange** can mean deceit and distrust.

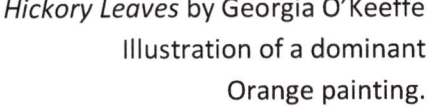

Hickory Leaves by Georgia O'Keeffe
Illustration of a dominant
Orange painting.

19

To mix the clearest orange, choose the two colors next to **ORANGE** on the color wheel. Notice that in both contributing colors they include the word **ORANGE**?

YELLOW-ORANGE   **RED-ORANGE**

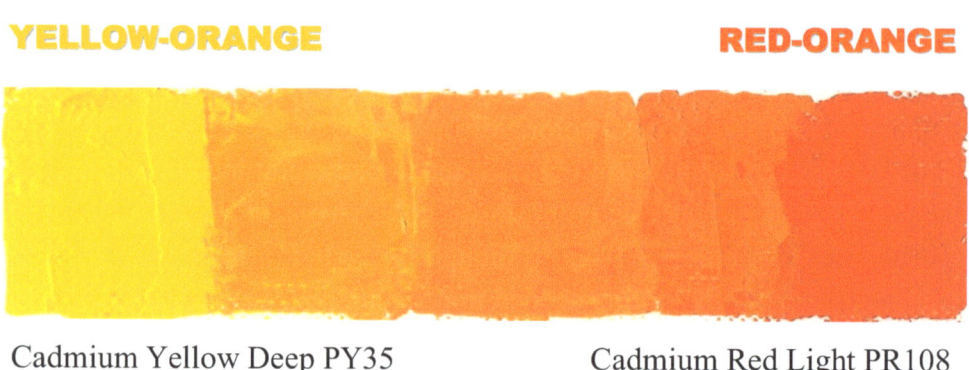

Cadmium Yellow Deep PY35   Cadmium Red Light PR108

The same **YELLOW-ORANGE** as above was used in this next illustration, but the **RED** was changed to a cooler mid red. By changing just the red to a deeper version, it changes the intensity or chroma of the **ORANGE**. Notice how the mid-section of this illustration is not as bright as the first example above.

YELLOW-ORANGE   **RED**

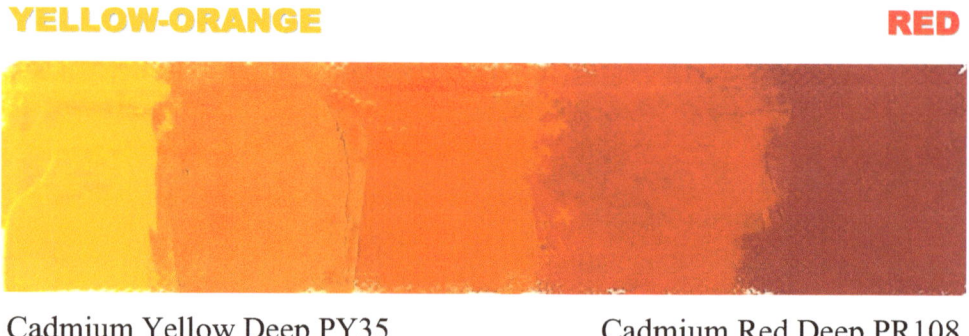

Cadmium Yellow Deep PY35   Cadmium Red Deep PR108

To illustrate further how the chroma of orange changes with different contributing colors, in the illustration below, the yellow was changed to a cool **YELLOW** and the cool mid **RED** was used again. These two colors are separated from **ORANGE** by one step each on the Color Wheel. Using this cool **YELLOW** and cool **RED**, places the bias of this **ORANGE** to a less chromatic, lighter version than the previous two illustrations.

YELLOW   **RED**

Hansa PY3   Cadmium Red Deep PR108

To create a neutral or low chroma orange, we chose a yellow and red that are each two steps away from **ORANGE** on the Color Wheel: **YELLOW-GREEN** as a cool yellow and **RED-VIOLET** as a cool red. This range of colors now looks similar to a Yellow Ochre to a Burnt Sienna. The orange has been neutralized by the blue bias in each of the contributing colors.

YELLOW-GREEN   **RED-VIOLET**

Mix of Hansa Yellow PY3 plus Phthalo Blue PB15   Permanent Alizarin Crimson PR177

GREEN

a cool Secondary Color—its Complementary color is RED

Phthalo Green PG7 and Viridian PG18 are the typical color pigment for this group. If your color scheme includes the use of Green, the bias may be important. If, for instance, there are more yellow tones in the picture, you may need to choose a green that has a stronger yellow bias. Create a series of sample color charts so you will know you are using the right green before you start your project.

Phthalo Green YS PG36 (left)   **Phthalo Green BS PG7** (right)

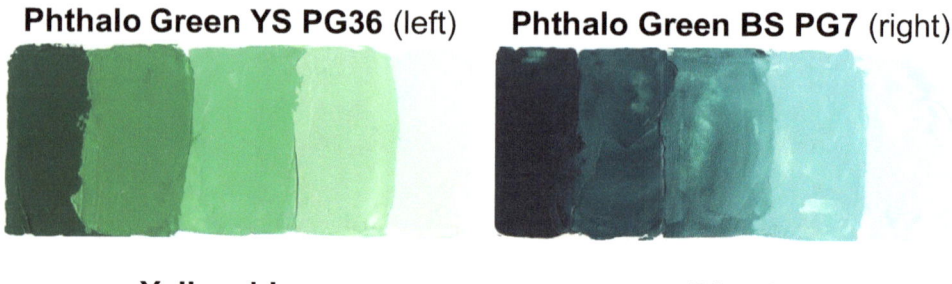

Yellow bias   **Blue bias**

GREEN tube color names with index numbers are Phthalo Green PG36, Phthalo Green PG7 and Viridian PG18.

Note on Green tube colors: Many Greens on the market are mixes using various pigments. If you use these pre-mixed greens, be sure the pigments listed on the tube are permanent colors. Pigments not considered permanent are called fugitives and will fade quickly.

Color names associated with GREEN are Chrome, Emerald, Kelly, and Permanent Green.

History

Green pigments have been used since Antiquity, both in the form of natural earth and malachite, used primarily by Egyptians. Greeks introduced verdigris, one of the first artificial pigments. Verdigris was introduced in European 15th century easel painting but was soon discarded. Copper resinate, made from verdigris, is not lightfast, even in oil paint. In the presence of light and air, green copper resinate becomes stable brown copper oxide. Until the 19th century, verdigris was the most vibrant green pigment available and was often used in painting. Thanks to chemistry, a new generation of greens was introduced beginning in the late 18th century: Cobalt green, Emerald green, and Viridian. Monet's use of Emerald Green pigment, which contained arsenic, may have contributed to his blindness in later life.

Physical and Emotional Interpretations

The most common associations to green are found in its ties to nature's powerful energies. Green grass is the most restful color. Green symbolizes self-respect, well-being, and is associated with regeneration, fertility, and rebirth. It is the color of balance and a sense of order. Green is a safe color; if you do not know what color to use anywhere use green. Green is considered the color of peace. It symbolizes a healthy environment and the renewal of spring in harmony with growth and tranquility. It is the color of the good luck (shamrock) and of generosity. Green is the merging of yellow (mind) and blue (spirit). It is found exactly at the point of color balance—midway between red and violet on the color spectrum. Culturally, green has broad and sometimes contradictory meanings. In some cultures, green symbolizes hope and growth, while in others it is associated with death, sickness, envy, or the devil. Green is the color of Friday.

Green is known to have signified witchcraft, devilry and evil and for its association with faeries and spirits of early English folklore. It also had an association with decay and toxicity. Recent political groups have taken on the color as symbol of environmental protection and social justice, and consider themselves part of the Green movement, some naming themselves Green parties. This has led to similar campaigns in advertising, as companies have sold green, or environmentally friendly, products. In areas that use the U.S. Dollar as currency, green carries a connotation of money, wealth, and capitalism, because green is the color of United States banknotes, giving rise to the slang term greenback for cash. Sometimes it can also describe someone who is inexperienced or jealous. Several connotations have derived from these meanings, such as "green around the gills", a phrase used to describe a person who looks ill and "green with envy", based on a line from Shakespeare's Othello.

More on Green

Green is so varied for landscapes. Manufacturers are always producing new variations and color names and you could not possibly stock all the greens available. Some of the colors used to make green are not lightfast such as Nitroso Green PG8 (also known as Hooker's Green) and Arylide Yellow PY1 found in Sap or Helio Green. Generally speaking, the greens offered by the paint companies are mixes of yellows and blues, so you need to be sure the contributing colors are labeled lightfast and permanent. Manufacturers report that using small amounts of these fugitive colors used in the colorfastness rating are minimal so they may justify giving them a higher lightfastness rating. Either way, you will have to make the determination yourself whether to risk its use or not. Less expensive ingredients are used in student grade paints and are often not lightfast and not suitable for longevity.

If you need to use a tube of "green" paint in your artwork, consider mixing it yourself pairing stable, lightfast colors. Lightfastness of color should be considered for permanent fine art.

I am primarily a landscape painter, but I avoid the use of green tube colors in my summer landscapes. There is a saying that artists call "falling into the *green trap*". This is understandable when painting a summer day where all appears to be filled with the greens of grass, trees and hills or mountains. To avoid monotonous use of green from a tube color, be sure to mix other colors into your green, varying the hues throughout the painting.

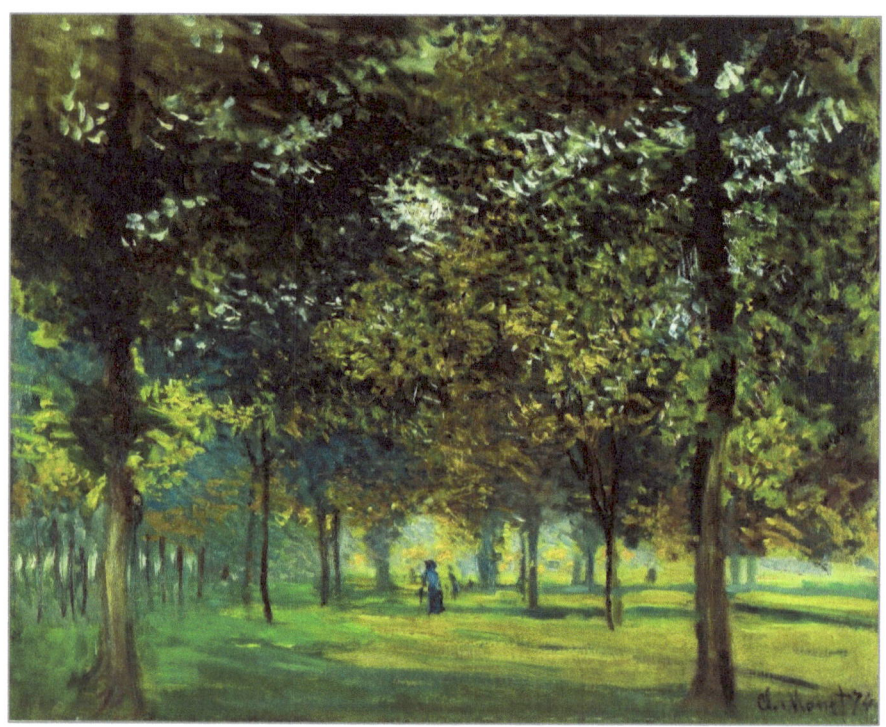

The Allee du Champ de Foire at Argenteuil by Claude Monet
Illustration of a dominant green painting.

MIXING GREEN

A varied range of greens can be mixed using various yellow and blue pigments as you will see in the following illustrations. If you need to produce a clear, bright green, your contributing colors need be closest to green itself. If a more neutralized or dull green is desired, then the two contributing colors need to be further from the GREEN. Try challenging yourself to mix your green rather than reaching for a tube. You will find that as you get in the habit of mixing your own green you will create strong harmony in your paintings. This series of illustrations will show you how the outcome of your green is largely dependent on the bias of each contributing color.

In the illustration below, both contributing colors have a strong green bias because they are adjacent colors to **GREEN** on the color wheel. It stands to reason that together; they will create the clearest brightest green.

Mix of Hansa Yellow PY3 plus Phthalo Blue PB15   Phthalo Blue PB15:3

In the illustration below, **YELLOW** has been changed, which helps produce a lighter high intensity yellow-green, but as it moves toward the **BLUE-GREEN** side, the darker color loses some of its intensity.

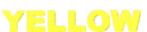

Hansa Yellow PY3   Phthalo Blue PB15:3

Yellow has been changed to a warmer **YELLOW-ORANGE** in the illustration below. See the shift to a duller green in comparison to the first two illustrations? This is due to the red bias in the **YELLOW-ORANGE**.

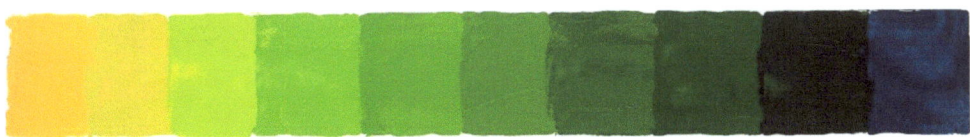

Cadmium Yellow Medium PY35   Phthalo Blue PB15:3

The illustration below it is not as bright as the **YELLOW-GREEN** and **BLUE-GREEN** illustration on the previous page. This is due to the slight red bias in the Cobalt Blue.

Mix of Hansa Yellow PY3 plus Phthalo Blue PB15 - Cobalt Blue Deep PB28

The illustration below uses contributing colors that are each <u>two</u> steps further away from **GREEN** on the color wheel. As they move away from **GREEN**, they begin to produce a color range moving toward a dull or neutral green.

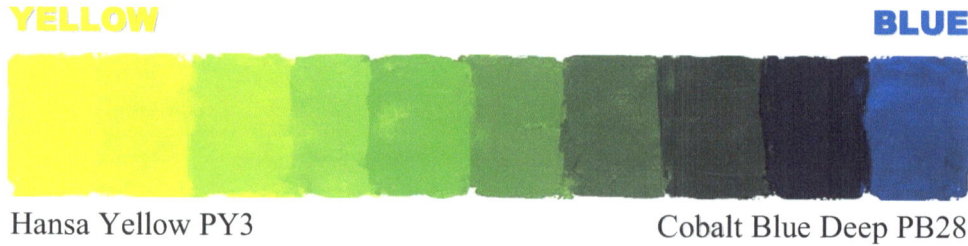

Hansa Yellow PY3   Cobalt Blue Deep PB28

Again, due to the red bias in the **YELLOW-ORANGE**, the middle color is now leaning toward what might be described as Chromium Oxide Green.

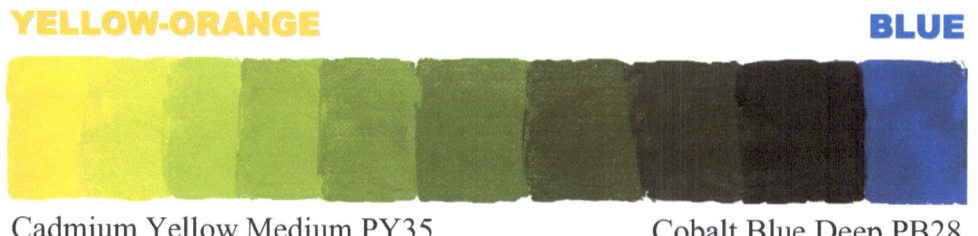

Cadmium Yellow Medium PY35   Cobalt Blue Deep PB28

BLUE-VIOLET has a red bias so using it as one of the contributing colors will produce a neutralized type of green. Even when the contributing yellow color has a blue bias, the red bias in the **BLUE-VIOLET** continues to neutralize the green and will still not be able to produce a bright green.

Mix of Hansa Yellow PY3 plus Phthalo Blue PB15 - Ultramarine Blue PB29

Are you starting to see what is happening to the **GREEN** each time you introduce a stronger red bias color to it? Below, the yellow has been changed to a more neutral, primary yellow, which allows the yellow-green colors to have a lighter chroma.

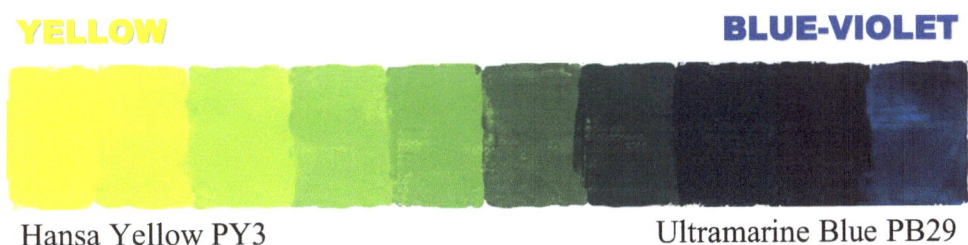

Hansa Yellow PY3   Ultramarine Blue PB29

As your contributing colors move further from **GREEN** they develop a more distant relationship. The middle green in the illustration below loses its' chroma or saturation now because both contributing colors, **YELLOW-ORANGE** and **BLUE-VIOLET**, have more red bias in each color than in any other illustration. This would be considered a low chroma or neutral green and may be described as a Golden or Sap Green.

Cadmium Yellow Medium PY35   Ultramarine Blue PB29

VIOLET
a cool Secondary Color—its Complementary color is YELLOW

Quinacridone Violet PV19 and Dioxazine Violet PV37 are both permanent color choices for this group. Below are two examples of different violet bias. The bias need of your tube violet may be different for each painting. Manufactured violets can range from a red shade (purple) to a blue shade (violet). Paint test colors to decide which color will be best for your painting.

Quinacridone Violet PV19 (left) or Dioxazine Violet PV37

Red bias   **Blue bias**

VIOLET tube color names with index numbers are Cobalt Violet PV14, Dioxazine Violet PV37, Manganese Violet PV16, Quinacridone Violet PV19 and PV42 and Ultramarine Violet PV15.

Color names associated with VIOLET are Cobalt Violet, Plum, Purple Madder, Raspberry and Ultramarine Violet.

History

Violet was named after the violet flower. It is synonymous with a bluish purple. When the word "purple" is used in the common English language, the sense of any color between blue and red comes to mind. Isaac Newton listed violet as his name for the color of the short-wavelength end of the visible spectrum. When both of the names *purple* and *violet* are used within the same system, *violet* represents colors nearer to blue, while *purple* is used for colors nearer to red on what is called, in color theory, the line of purples. The first recorded use of *violet* as a color name in English was in 1370.

Physical and Emotional Interpretations

Violet is the color of good judgment, generosity, health, and fertility. It is the color of people seeking enlightenment, spiritual fulfillment, and wisdom. It is said if you surround yourself with violet, you will have peace of mind. Violet is a good color to use in meditation and renewal. In Chinese painting, the color violet stands for the *harmony of the universe* because it is a combination of red and blue. It is used by royalty and nobility and can be dignified and sophisticated. In the United Kingdom it is traditional to package chocolate in violet colored packaging because of the association with the color royal purple. The combination of red and blue, violet is believed to be the ideal color. Most children love the color violet so it can stand for youth. Red brings practicality to the undirected expansiveness of the blue and allows more creative energy to emerge. For this reason, violet is associated with imagination and inspiration and is the color most favored by artists. Violet has been used to symbolize magic, fantasy, and mystery. Thursday's color is Violet.

The negative trait of Violet is arrogance and cruelty. It can be filled with envy, jealousy, and misfortune.

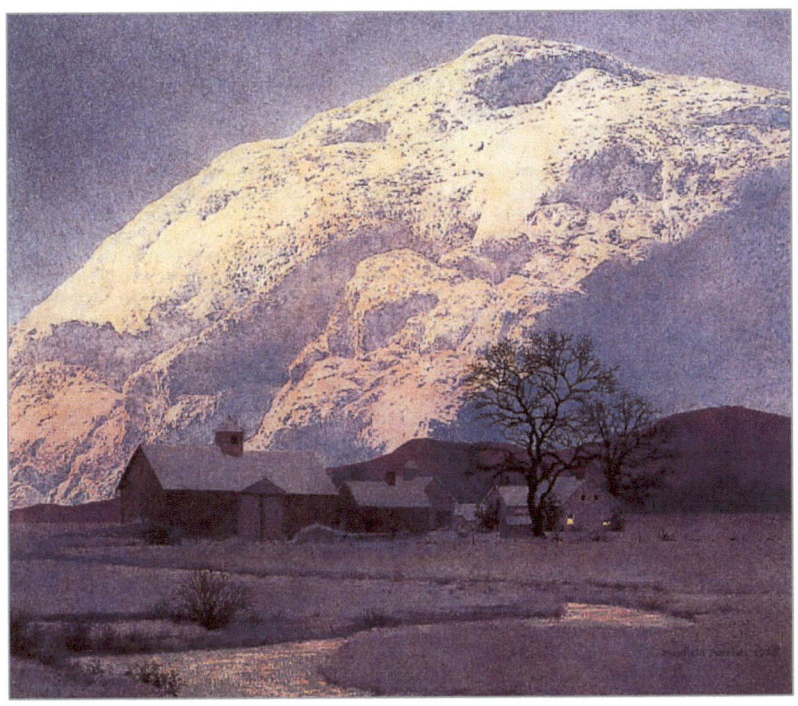

Mountain Farm at Winter by Maxfield Parrish
Illustration of a dominant Violet painting.

MIXING VIOLET

Manufacturers produce the desired bias they choose, and some cheaper versions may have a mix of red and blue to produce a facsimilies of violet. The pure violet pigment, Cobalt Violet PV14 is relatively expensive. Ultramarine Violet PV15, Quinacridone Violet PV19 and Dioxazine Violet available as PV23 or PV37 are all less expensive alternatives. Violet PV23, is said to have a less permanent rating than PV37, so PV37 would be a better choice for permanent work. Because the pigments in the illustrations below are so dark, white has been added on the second row, for better identification of the color.

To make a clear bright violet you will use the two colors next to **VIOLET** on the Color Wheel. Using a bright red-violet (Magenta PR122) aids in making this a beautiful violet.

RED-VIOLET   **BLUE-VIOLET**

Magenta PR122   Ultramarine Blue PB29

Changing the **RED-VIOLET** to a bluer bias shade (Perm. Alizarin Crimson PR177) and using the same **BLUE-VIOLET**, as in the illustration below, you can see how the result produces a deeper **VIOLET**.

RED-VIOLET   **BLUE-VIOLET**

Permanent Alizarin Crimson PR177   Ultramarine Blue PB29

Typically, we think of mixing red and blue to make a violet, but by observing the different bias in the red and blue that are chosen in the next examples, you can see how it affects the violet color bias. The bias of violet will also have a predetermined outcome, based on the colors in a scheme you choose.

To make a less intense violet, use contributing colors that are two color steps away from **VIOLET** on the Color Wheel. The more you change the contributing colors to have a bias toward its complementary, the more your color will be neutralized.

RED   **BLUE**

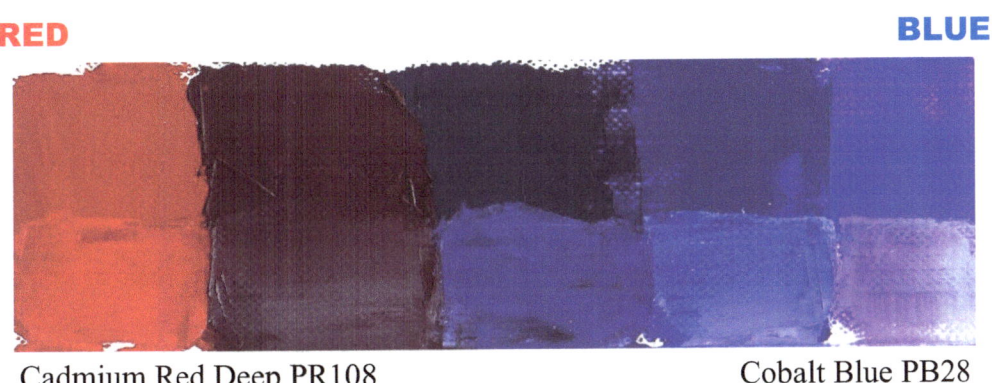

Cadmium Red Deep PR108   Cobalt Blue PB28

To mix a gray violet, or as I prefer to call it, a neutral **VIOLET**, use a red and blue, both with a strong yellow bias as in the illustration below. You can see how the middle color is a very neutral color in comparison to the previous illustrations.

RED-ORANGE   **BLUE-GREEN**

Cadmium Red Light PR108   Phthalo Blue PB15

You can practice this idea by just changing one of the colors but not the other.

TERTIARY COLORS

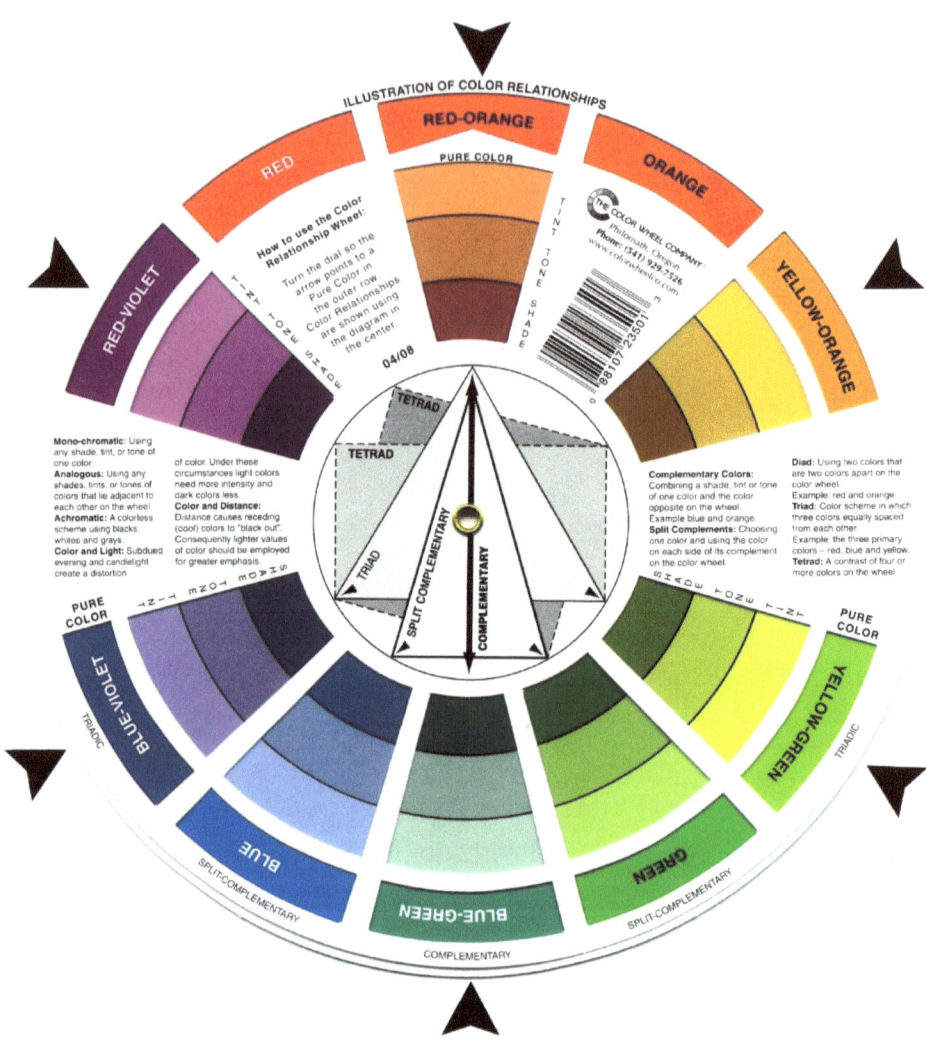

ILLUSTRATION OF COLOR RELATIONSHIPS

How to use the Color Relationship Wheel:

Turn the dial so the arrow points to a Pure Color in the outer row. Color Relationships are shown using the diagram in the center.

04/08

THE COLOR WHEEL COMPANY
Philomath, Oregon
Phone: (541) 929-7526
www.colorwheelco.com

Mono-chromatic: Using any shade, tint, or tone of one color
Analogous: Using any shades, tints, or tones of colors that lie adjacent to each other on the wheel.
Achromatic: A colorless scheme using blacks, whites and grays.
Color and Light: Subdued evening and candlelight create a distortion

of color. Under these circumstances light colors need more intensity and dark colors less.
Color and Distance:
Distance causes receding (cool) colors to "black out". Consequently lighter values of color should be employed for greater emphasis.

Complementary Colors:
Combining a shade, tint or tone of one color and the color opposite on the wheel. Example blue and orange.
Split Complements: Choosing one color and using the color on each side of its complement on the color wheel

Diad: Using two colors that are two colors apart on the color wheel.
Example: red and orange.
Triad: Color scheme in which three colors equally spaced from each other.
Example: the three primary colors - red, blue and yellow.
Tetrad: A contrast of four or more colors on the wheel.

TERTIARY COLORS

Tertiary: \'ter-shē,er-ē

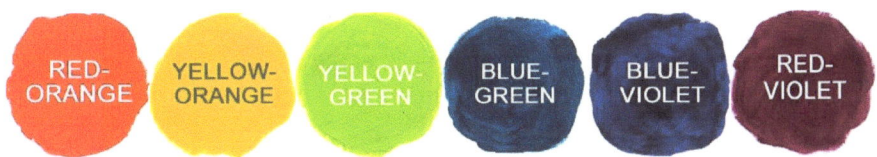

Tertiary colors are combined names of a primary and secondary color therefore having a double word name. These colors make up half of the twelve color groups on the Color Wheel.

When mixing tertiary colors, be sure your contributing tube colors have only one pure color pigment so you can fully understand their bias..

Like the secondary colors, the pure tube versions of a Tertiary color can offer more brilliant color choices than from pre-mixed.

Using the Tertiary Colors in a Triad color scheme may offer some interesting mixes. A Triad of Tertiary colors is worth exploring as a color scheme.

A Split Primary color scheme uses all the Tertiary colors. Another way to think about it is that these colors are the warm and cool of each primary color.

RED-ORANGE

a warm Tertiary Color—its Complementary color is BLUE-GREEN

RED-ORANGE is traditionally interpreted as Cadmium Red Light PR108. The examples below are Cadmium Red Light but have a different bias. Choose the color bias based on the need. Example: if there is a bias of orange in your painting you may need to choose a RED-ORANGE that has more yellow bias.

Cadmium Red Light PR108

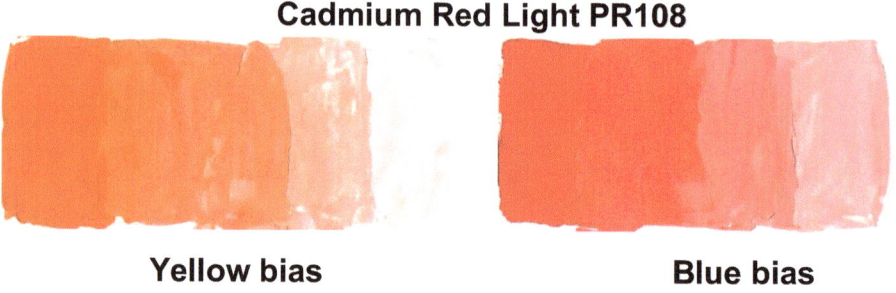

Yellow bias   **Blue bias**

RED-ORANGE tube color names with index numbers are Cadmium Red Light PR108, Naphthol Red PR112 and Pyrrole Scarlet PR255.

Color names associated with RED-ORANGE are China Red, Chinese, Helio, Permanent, Scarlet and Vermilion.

History

Vermilion PR106 is an opaque RED-ORANGE pigment that has been used since antiquity. Most naturally produced vermilion is derived from Cinnabar, an ore having high levels of mercury commonly found in China, giving its alternative name of China Red. Vermilion, was favored for its deep RED-ORANGE color by old master painters such as Titian. It has been replaced in painters' palettes by more stable modern pigments, including the Cadmium Red Light PR101. Although genuine Vermilion PR106 paint can still be bought for fine arts and art conservation applications, few manufacturers are producing it any longer due to legal liability issues over the toxicity levels. As a result, genuine Vermilion PR106 is almost unavailable. Today, vermilion is most commonly artificially produced, and is properly designated as Vermilion Hue to distinguish it from genuine Vermilion PR106.

Physical and Emotional Interpretations

The positive side of RED-ORANGE corresponds to desire, joy, sexual passion, sensitivity, love and pleasure. RED-ORANGE is a bright vibrant color which symbolizes physical energy.

The negative side to RED-ORANGE is aggression, domination and thirst for action.

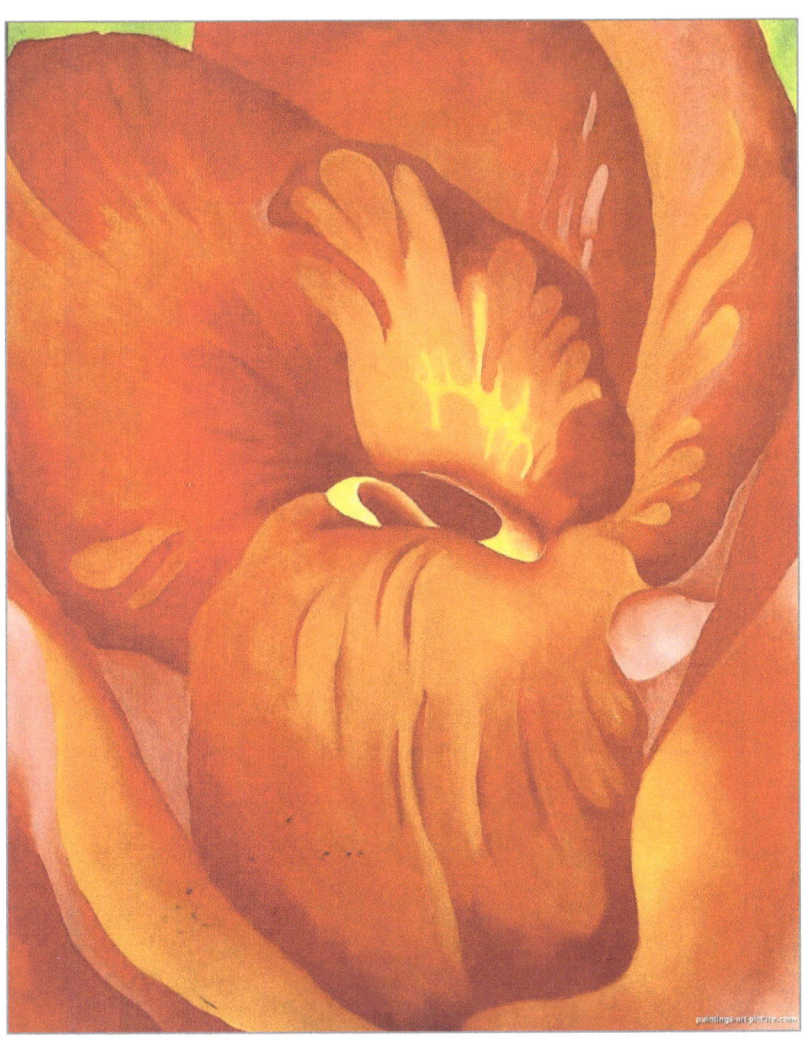

Canna by Georgia O'Keeffe
Illustration of a dominant Red-Orange painting.

35

YELLOW-ORANGE

a warm Tertiary color—its Complementary color is BLUE-VIOLET

Cadmium Yellow PY35 is the artist's traditional YELLOW-ORANGE and is available in light, medium, and dark shades which come close to resembling Orange. It is brilliant, dense, and opaque, with very good hiding power. The YELLOW-ORANGE color group is light in value and is sometimes difficult to show its bias. Manufacturers offer light versions by adding white to the color.

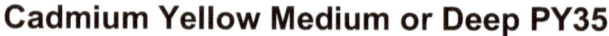

Cadmium Yellow Medium or Deep PY35

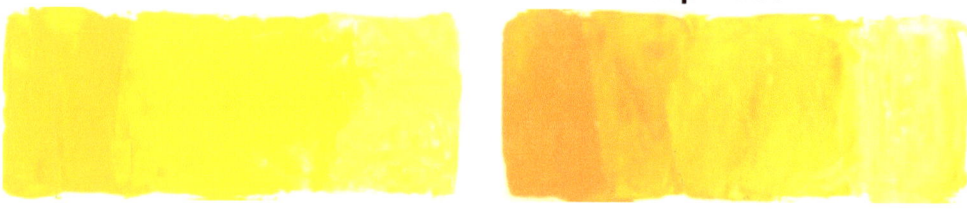

Blue bias   **Red bias**

YELLOW-ORANGE tube color names with index numbers are Cadmium Yellow Medium or Deep PY35, Hansa Yellow Deep PY65 and Nickel Dioxime Yellow PY153.

Color names associated with YELLOW-ORANGE are Cadmium Yellow, Gamboge, Indian Yellow and Permanent Yellow.

History

Oil colors were first made from Cadmium yellow pigments in 1819, replacing toxic Chrome (lead) Yellows. Their production was delayed until 1840 due to the scarcity of cadmium metals. Landscape painters, such as Claude Monet, preferred Cadmium Yellow to the less expensive Chrome Yellow because of its higher chroma and greater purity of color.

In some of Vincent van Gogh's paintings, the yellow he used has dulled to coffee-brown, and in about 10 of them, the discoloration is serious, said Koen Janssens, an analytical chemist at Antwerp University in Belgium who co-authored the study. The root of the problem is the yellow lead chromate paint he used. Chrome paints were far brighter and more vibrant than earlier yellow. Visit the website referenced at back of this book for the full story.

Physical and Emotional Interpretations

Gold evokes the feeling of prestige. The meaning of gold is illumination, wisdom, and wealth. It is sensitive to criticism. Gold often symbolizes high quality. Yellow-Gold is Sunday's color.

Golden Yellow is the color of the loner with an intense curiosity and interest in investigating the finer details of life's interests. The darker shades of yellow show an inclination toward depression and melancholy, lack of love and low self-worth. Dark yellow relates to the constant complainer and the cynic.

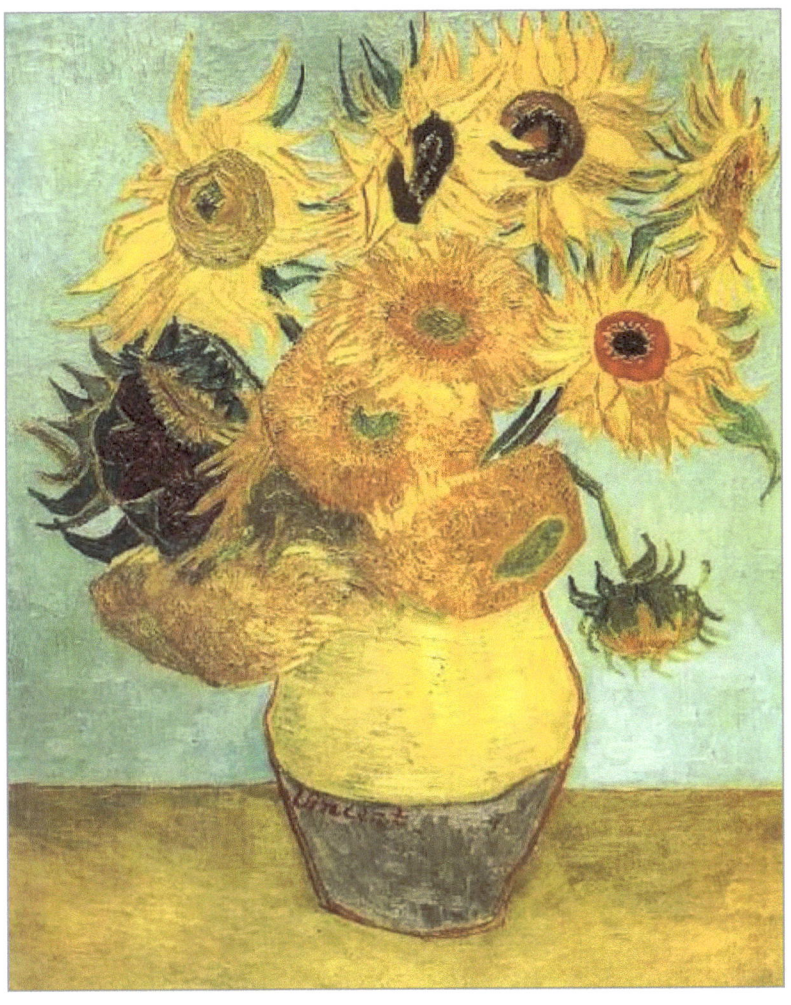

Sunflowers by Vincent van Gogh
Illustration of a dominant Yellow-Orange painting.

YELLOW-GREEN

a warm Tertiary Color—its Complementary color is RED-VIOLET

YELLOW-GREEN is the only color on the Color Wheel not found as a single pigment. It is a blend of multiple mixed color pigments with the bias decided by each manufacturer. When buying this tube color, choose those that have permanent pigments in the ingredients. This color is often labeled as Permanent Yellow Green. Mix your own YELLOW-GREEN with Phthalo Blue PB15:3 or Phthalo Green PG7 and Cadmium Lemon PY35 or Hansa Yellow PY3 for the brightest YELLOW-GREEN. These are my choice of ingredients because they are all permanent colors.

When using YELLOW-GREEN in your color scheme, you may need its bias to be more yellow than green, especially if the YELLOW-GREEN will be your sole YELLOW in the color scheme. If the YELLOW-GREEN you have purchased has more of a green bias to it, you may need to add YELLOW to it (Hansa PY3 or Lemon yellow PY35) to achieve the bias you need. Test your YELLOW-GREEN by adding white to it to better identify the bias.

If you cannot find a satisfactory blend in a tube color, you can mix your own YELLOW-GREEN and store in an empty tube found at online art supply stores.

Permanent Yellow Green (contains various pigments)

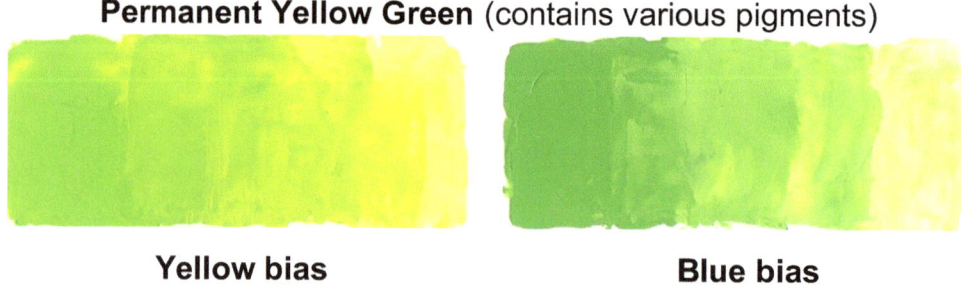

Yellow bias　　　　　　　　　**Blue bias**

Color names associated with YELLOW-GREEN are Apple, Chartreuse, Lime, Moss, Neon, Olive and Sap green.

History

Chartreuse is the color precisely halfway between green and yellow. Chartreuse was one of the original names coming from its resemblance to the green color of one of the French liqueurs called *green chartreuse*, introduced in 1764. Similarly, *chartreuse yellow* is a yellow color mixed with a small amount of green that was named because of its resemblance to the color of one of the French liqueurs called *yellow chartreuse*, introduced in 1838. The first recorded use of *lime green* as a color name in English was in 1905.

Physical and Emotional Interpretations

Yellow-Green allows us to be perceptive and nonjudgmental. This color inspires us to try new things by initiating change.

The negative side of Yellow-Green can mean deceit and creates a disoriented feeling.

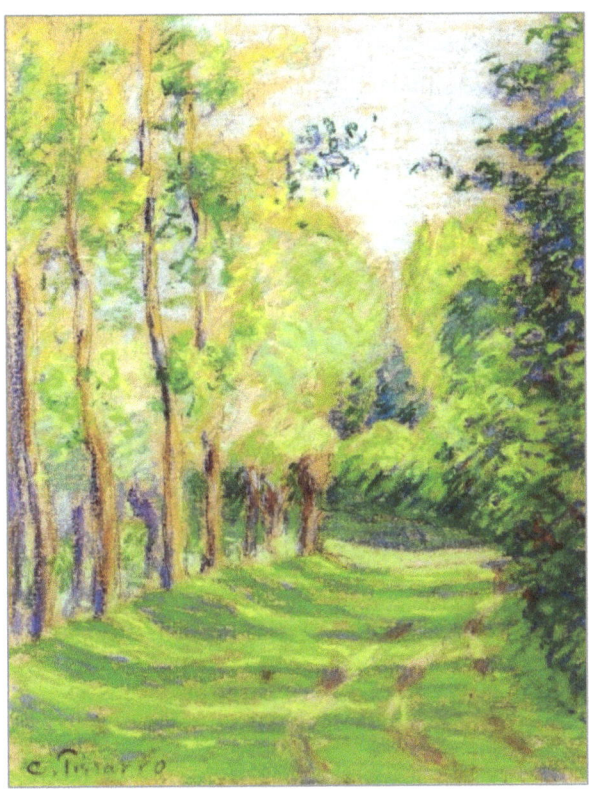

Landscape at Saint Charles by Camille Pissarro
Illustration of a dominant Yellow-Green painting.

BLUE GREEN

a cool Tertiary Color—its Complementary color is RED-ORANGE

The BLUE-GREEN tube pigment is often found as Phthalocyanine Blue PB15. Typically found in a red shade (RS) PB15:1 and a green shade (GS) PB15:3. If the pigment is listed with no suffix PB15, assume it to be the red shade (RS). Phthalo pigment is an intense blue but extremely versatile color.

Phthalo Blue GS PB15:3 (left) or Phthalo Blue RS PB15 or 15:1 (right)

Yellow bias   **Red bias**

BLUE-GREEN tube color names with index numbers are Cerulean Blue PB35, Cobalt Chromite PB36, Heliogen Blue PB16, Phthalocyanine Blue PB15(GS), 15:1(GS), 15:2 or 15:3(RS), and Phthalocyanine Cyan PB17.

Color names associated with BLUE-GREEN are Aqua, Aquamarine, Cerulean, Cyan, Manganese, Phthalocyanine (Phthalo or Thalo), Prussian, Teal and Turquoise.

History

Cyan comes from the Romanization of the Greek word *kýanos,* loosely translated as "dark blue substance". It may be used as the name of any of a number of colors in the BLUE-GREEN range of the spectrum. Cyan is also one of the common inks used in four-color printing, along with magenta, yellow, and black; this set of colors is referred to as CMYK. BLUE-GREEN is thought of by some as the Primary Blue color.

Maxfield Parrish was very fond of the Cyan pigment as an illustrator and most of his color palettes included the CMYK colors exclusively.

Phthalocyanine blue PB15, also known as Monastral blue, was first developed as a pigment in the mid-1930s. Its brilliant blue is often used in paints and dyes. Due to its stability, Phthalo blue is also used in inks, coatings, and many plastics.

Prussian blue PB27 was the first modern synthetic pigment, discovered by accident in 1704. By the early 19th century, synthetic and metallic blue pigments had been added to the range of blues.

Physical and Emotional Interpretations

Turquoise is the symbol of youth. This color has a soothing effect. Turquoise is the color of communication. Turquoise has long been used in good luck charms to provide protection, health, confidence, and strength. It radiates the peace, calm and tranquility of blue and the balance and growth of green. It recharges our spirits during times of mental stress. Turquoise is slightly greener than Cyan.

Too much Turquoise and we can become over-analytical, fussy, and egocentric. It can lead to either over-emotional or non-emotional imbalance.

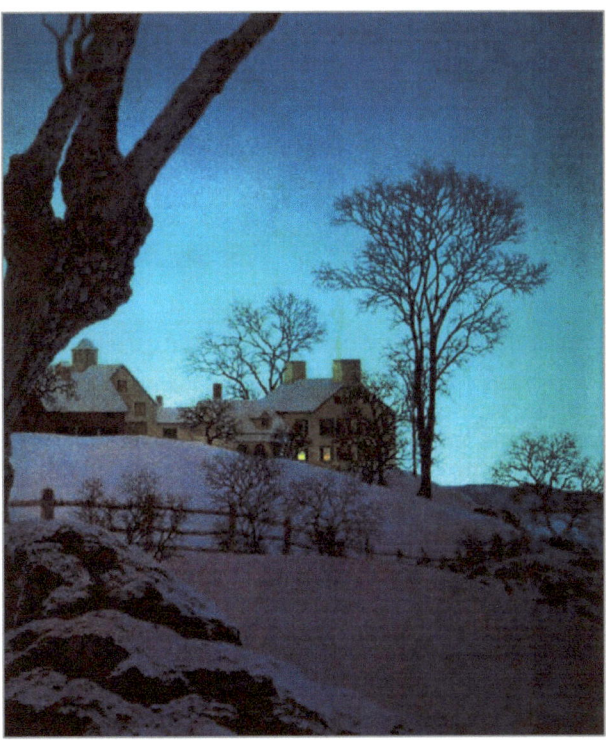

Christmas Morning by Maxfield Parrish
Illustration of a dominant
Blue-Green painting.

BLUE-VIOLET

a cool Tertiary Color—its Complementary color is YELLOW-ORANGE

BLUE-VIOLET as found in Ultramarine Blue PB29 is one of the few truer BLUE-VIOLET colors. BLUE-VIOLET hues vary slightly, and variations generally tend to be less noticeable than in other colors. As with all the dark colors, you will need to add white to really see the bias of the color more clearly.

Ultramarine Blue PB29

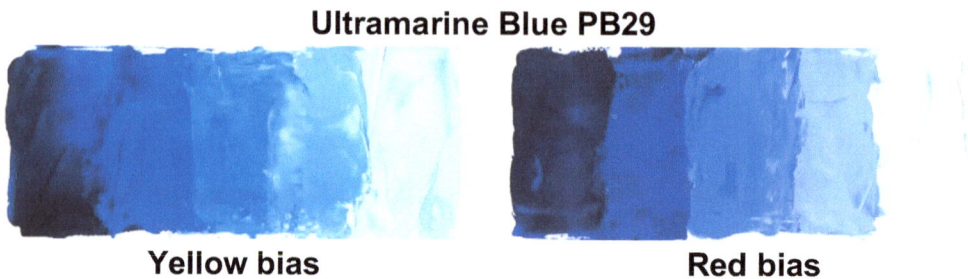

Yellow bias   **Red bias**

BLUE-VIOLET tube color names with index numbers are Indanthrene Blue PB60, Indigo PB66 and Ultramarine Blue PB29.

Color names associated with BLUE-VIOLET are Azurite, Indigo, Lapis Lazuli, French Ultramarine Blue, and Ultramarine Blue.

History

Lapis lazuli (pronounced *LAP-iss LAZ-ew-lye/lee*) and sometimes abbreviated to lapis, is a relatively rare semi-precious stone that has been prized since antiquity for its intense blue color. Lapis lazuli is often referred to as Ultramarine Blue getting the name in parts from *ultra*, meaning *beyond*, and *mare*, meaning *sea*, because it was imported from Asia to Europe by sea. It was one of the most expensive pigments in 16th century Europe, worth twice its weight in gold, and so was used sparingly and when commissions were larger. Lapis lazuli was, and still is, an extraordinary and expensive pigment for artists, a color of luxury. Lapis lazuli has been mined from mines in the Badakhshan province of Afghanistan for over 6,000 years and there are sources that are found as far east as Siberia. Other mines are found in Argentina, Chile, Myanmar (formerly Burma), Pakistan, and the U.S. (California). It is rare but still available for purchase as a paint pigment. One of the most famous paintings where it was used is the "Girl with the Pearl Earring" by Johannes Vermeer.

Synthetic Ultramarine Blue PB29 is today quite widely used as an artist's pigment and is known to many as "French Ultramarine" PB29 because of its discovery (1830) and long production in France. French Ultramarine PB29 was adopted as a means of identifying the synthetic form from lapis lazuli. Some manufacturers adhere to this but not always.

Indigoid Blue PB66 (Indigo) is the famous blue dye used in many blue jeans and other denim products, famous for the way it fades! Although a few paint manufacturers offer a genuine Indigo PB66 color, it should be used only for applications that are not permanent, or where the color is needed for historical reasons.

Physical and Emotional Interpretations

Indigo amplifies the energy of blue in a profound way. At a physical level, while blue is calming, indigo is sedating. Indigo symbolizes a mystical borderland of wisdom, self-mastery, and spiritual realization. Indigo is the color of the deep midnight sky.

While BLUE is the color of communication with others, Indigo turns the blue inward, to increase personal thought, profound insights, and instant understandings. Indigo is almost instantaneous. Inventors use Indigo skills for inspirations that seem to 'come out of the blue'.

Indigo can have a negative effect when used during a depressed state, because it will deepen the mood.

Lapis lazuli and azurite are said to heighten psychic powers. The ancient Egyptians used lapis lazuli to represent heaven.

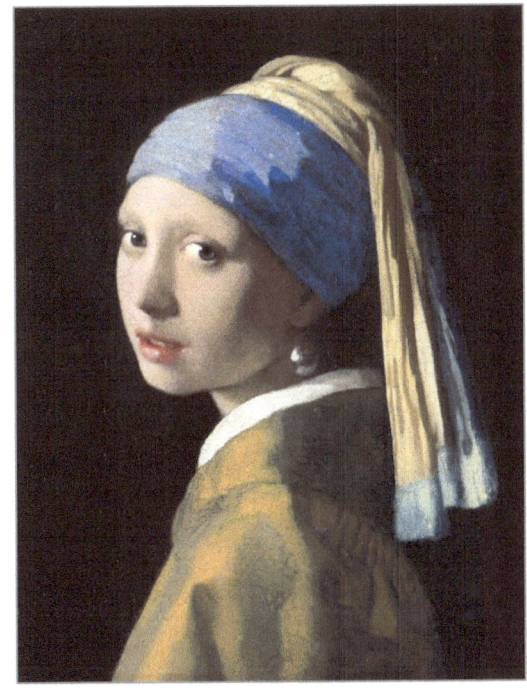

Girl with a Pearl Earring by Johannas Vermeer
Illustration of a dominant Blue-Violet painting.

RED-VIOLET

a warm Tertiary Color—its Complementary color is YELLOW-GREEN

The RED-VIOLET group has one of the most diverse hues among the color groups and is notably very intense, staining, and transparent. They can range from a vibrant color like Magenta PR122, useful for flowers, to a cool bluish, less intense color like Perylene Maroon PR179, which may be useful to neutralize green in a landscape. Add white to reveal its true bias.

Quinacridone Red PR122 (left) **Anthraquinone Red PR177** (right)

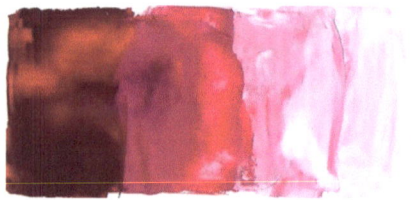 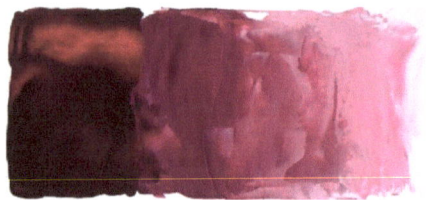

Yellow bias   **Blue bias**

RED-VIOLET tube color names with index numbers are Anthraquinone Red PR177, Perylene Maroon PR179 (Permanent Alizarin Crimson), Pyrrole Red Rubine PR264, Quinacridone Burnt Scarlet PR206 and Quinacridone Red (Magenta) PR122.

Color names associated with RED-VIOLET are Alizarin, Burgundy, Crimson, Mauve and Magenta.

History

The Madder plant has been cultivated as a dyestuff since antiquity in central Asia and Egypt, where it was grown as early as 1500 BC. In the middle Ages, Charlemagne encouraged madder cultivation. It grew well in the sandy soils of the Netherlands and became an important part of the local economy.

By 1804, the English dye maker George Field had refined the technique to lake madder. This resulting lake madder had a longer-lasting color, and it can be used more easily for blending it into paint.

In 1826, the French chemist Pierre-Jean Robiquet found that madder root had two colorants, the red alizarin and the more rapidly fading purpurin. The alizarin component became the first natural dye to be synthetically duplicated in 1868. Synthetic Alizarin could be produced for a fraction of the cost of the natural product, and the market for madder collapsed virtually overnight. Alizarin Crimson PR83 itself has been in turn largely replaced today by the more light-resistant Quinacridone pigments developed at DuPont in 1958. Alizarin Crimson PR83 has been the subject of much controversy and discussion in the art community about its use since it is prone to fading and darkening over time. When using this paint color name, be sure the labeling has the word "Permanent" associated with it. The pigment in these tubes should be made with a stable color like Anthraquinone Red PR177 or Perylene Maroon PR179.

The origin of Magenta was discovered in 1859 and named Fuchsine, made from coal tar dyes. The name of the color was soon changed from Fuchsine to Magenta, being named after the 1859 Battle of Magenta fought at Magenta (due to the color of the land covered by the blood of the casualties of the battle), Lombardy-Italy. The Magenta name is used to describe a color rather than being from pigment or dyes. Printer's magenta was invented in the 1890's for the CMYK printing process and the electric magenta for computer display was formulated in 1980. Both colors were artificially engineered.

Physical and Emotional Interpretations

To psychics who claim to be able to see the aura with their third eye, someone who has a magenta aura is usually described as being artistic and creative. It is reported that typical occupations for someone with a magenta aura would be such professions as artist, art dealer, actor, author, costume designer, or set designer.

When Magenta is out of balance, it might promote depression and despair in some and prevent others from dealing with challenges. Magenta is selfless and may have issues of not being grounded, focused, or having no concerns of one's own needs in life.

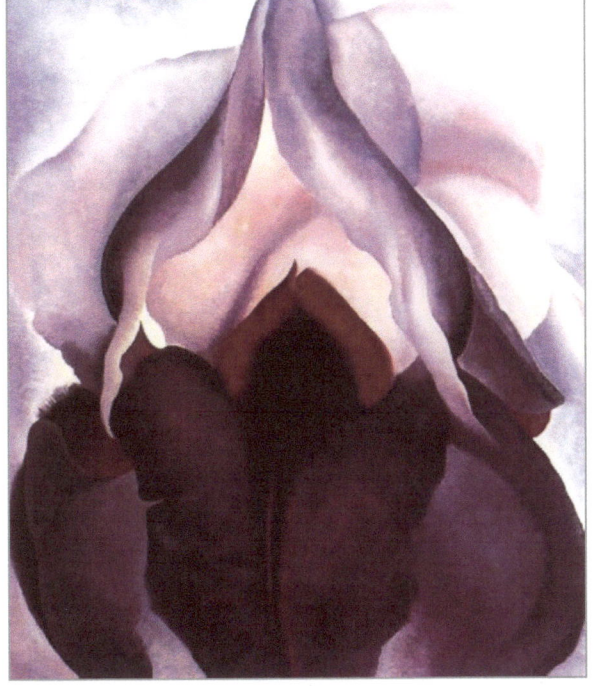

Flower of Life II
by Georgia O'Keeffe
Illustration of a dominant
Red-Violet painting.

High Intensity Colors
Light, Bright Colors

These colors work well to achieve a cheerful mood and are also considered feminine. Some manufacturers offer a high intensity color made by mixing a pure color with another high intensity color or tinted with white. You might even try mixing your own variations. Control the values of a high intensity painting by including accents of a middle and dark value color.

The following is a suggested list of high intensity colors with a single pigment and good lightfastness rating, for each color group.

RED; Naphthol AS-D PR112 or Pyrrole Red PR254.

RED-ORANGE; Pyrrole Scarlet PR255, or Naphthol Scarlet Lake PR188.

ORANGE; Pyrrol Orange PO73.

YELLOW-ORANGE; Hansa Yellow Deep PY65, Cadmium Yellow Light PY34.

YELLOW; Hansa Yellow PY3 or Cadmium Yellow Light PY35.

YELLOW-GREEN; Yellow-Green (mix).

GREEN; Cobalt Green PG26, Titanate Green PG50 or Permanent Light Green (various mix).

BLUE-GREEN; Cerulean Blue PB35.

BLUE; Cobalt Blue Light PB28 or Cobalt Chromite PB36

BLUE-VIOLET Ultramarine Blue Light PB29.

VIOLET; Cobalt Violet PV14 or Cobalt Lithium Violet Phosphate PV47.

RED-VIOLET; Quinacridone Red PR209 or Pigment Red PR221.

Brown, Earth and Neutral Colors

Brown, Earth or Neutral Colors are colors not readily identified on the Color Wheel but if you look closely, you can find a facsimile through the shade area on the back of the Color Wheel to classify them into. As the example below points out, Burnt Sienna might be classified anywhere between a RED through an ORANGE and Yellow Ochre might be classified as YELLOW-ORANGE.

Although I am not big on using earth pigments myself, it is worth looking at the range of colors they can produce. Further examples can be found in Chapter 5, Triad color schemes.

Physical and Emotional Interpretations

BROWN is associated with autumn, comfort, dependability, earth, endurance, grounded, heart, home, masculinity, qualities, natural, order, outdoors, reliability, simplicity, and stability.

REDDISH BROWN is associated with harvest and fall.

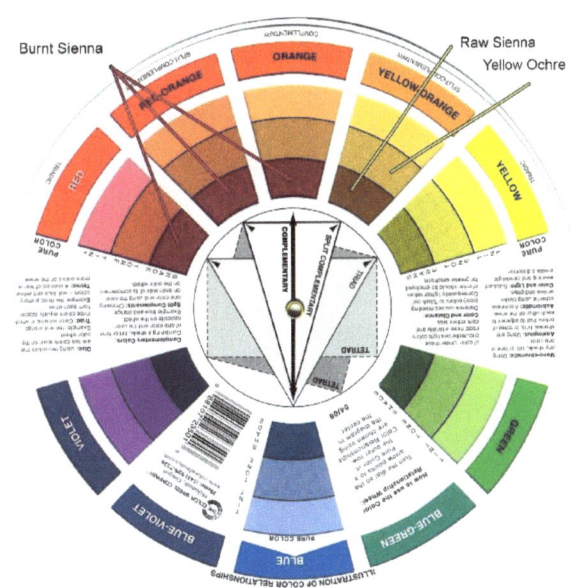

Low Intensity Colors

Dull Colors

Low Intensity colors can be classified into each of the twelve colors on the Color Wheel. They can also be mixed to create browns, earth, and neutral colors. Use a palette of low intensity tube colors together to create a low intensity painting.

See page 79 in the paperback version, for painting illustration using a High and Low Intensity color palettes.

The following is a suggested list of Low Intensity colors with a single pigment and good lightfastness rating, for each color group.

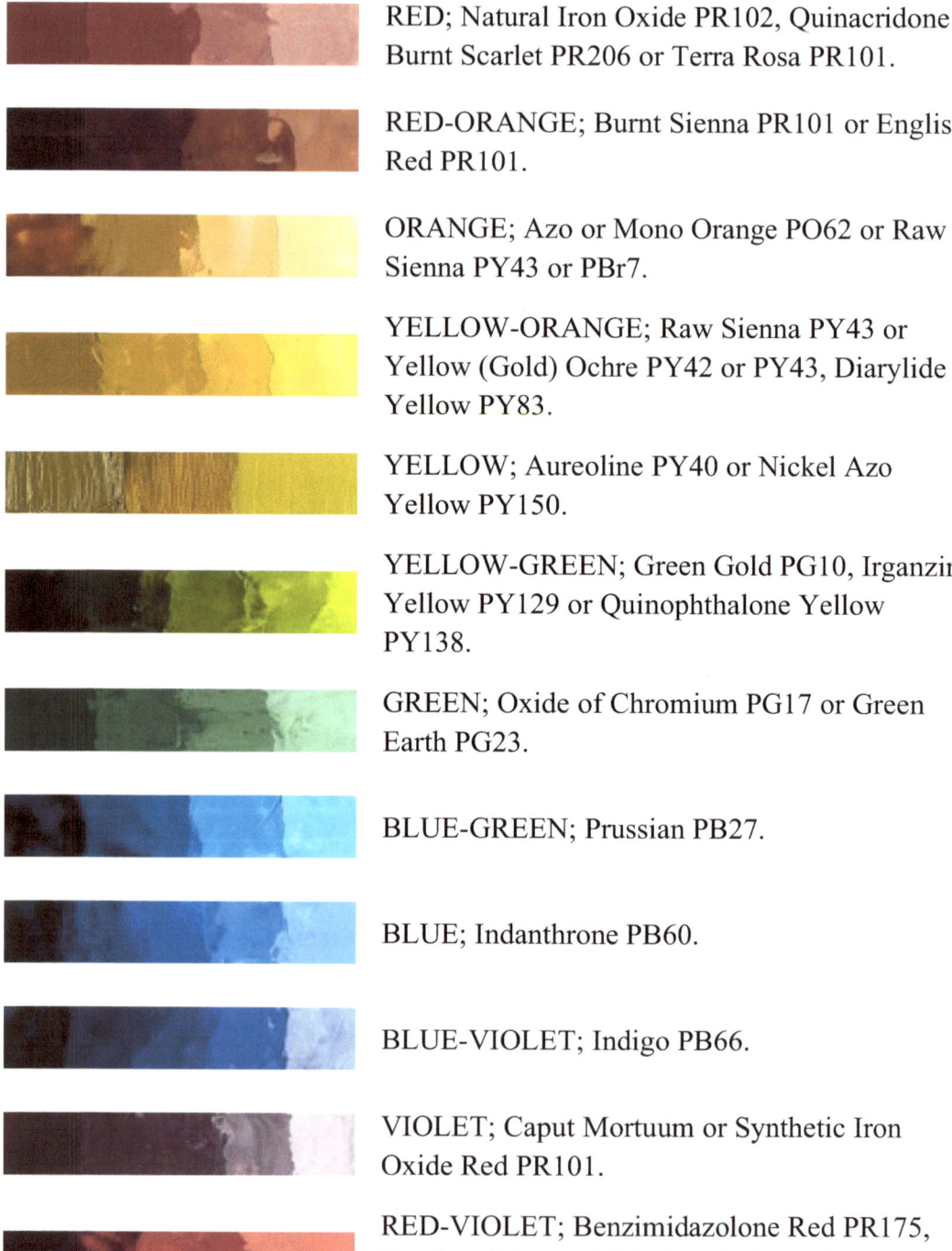

RED; Natural Iron Oxide PR102, Quinacridone Burnt Scarlet PR206 or Terra Rosa PR101.

RED-ORANGE; Burnt Sienna PR101 or English Red PR101.

ORANGE; Azo or Mono Orange PO62 or Raw Sienna PY43 or PBr7.

YELLOW-ORANGE; Raw Sienna PY43 or Yellow (Gold) Ochre PY42 or PY43, Diarylide Yellow PY83.

YELLOW; Aureoline PY40 or Nickel Azo Yellow PY150.

YELLOW-GREEN; Green Gold PG10, Irganzin Yellow PY129 or Quinophthalone Yellow PY138.

GREEN; Oxide of Chromium PG17 or Green Earth PG23.

BLUE-GREEN; Prussian PB27.

BLUE; Indanthrone PB60.

BLUE-VIOLET; Indigo PB66.

VIOLET; Caput Mortuum or Synthetic Iron Oxide Red PR101.

RED-VIOLET; Benzimidazolone Red PR175, Perylene Maroon PR179 or Quinacridone Maroon PV42.

Chapter 3

WHAT'S IN YOUR TUBE?

(THE TECHNICAL STUFF)

ASTM Labeling

The best way to learn about what is in your tubes of paint is to examine the labels. Just like food labels, the information on these labels is there for a reason.

The ASTM (American Society for Testing and Materials) was established in 1898. ASTM International provides a global forum for the development and publication of international voluntary consensus standards for materials, products, systems, and services. Known for their high technical quality and market relevance, the ASTM standards are used in research and development, product testing and quality systems. ASTM standards are a crucial element of the information infrastructure that guides manufacturing and trade in the global economy

To conform to the ASTM labeling standards, manufacturers must also use the designation "hue, extra or tint" for a paint that is named with a pigments' common name but that does not actually contain the pigment. They can be colors that have been mixed using multiple combinations of pigment ingredients including synthetically produced pigments producing a color that is intended to match a pure color. Example: Cadmium Red is an organic pigment called cadmium sulphoselenide with the Color Index name of PR108. The Cadmium Red Hue by Grumbacher contains Hansa Yellow PY74, Perylene Red PR149, Naphthol Red PR170 and Red Iron Oxide PR102. You can see that this Cadmium Red Hue does not include any Cadmium Red at all. Some manufacturers create their own signature line of colors such as Old Holland's *Scheveningen* or Winsor & Newton's, which are labeled as *Winsor*, plus the color name which is appropriate. This is where the color index name and numbers help to clear up the confusion.

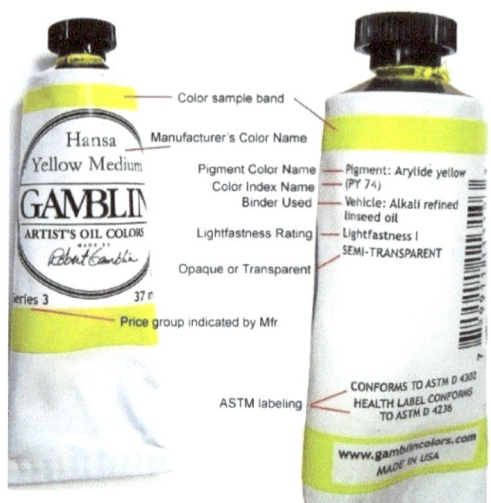

Alternative Names

These are names made up by the manufacturers. Although paint manufacturers have become more forthright, you cannot depend on paint manufacturers to name paints accurately. With the color index name, you cut through the marketing clutter and actually see what you're getting for your money.

Always refer to the color index name to be sure of what you are buying, and only choose paints that show the pigment common name and color index name on the tube: "Dioxazine Violet, PV37" (not Pansy Purple) and "Cadmium Red, PR108" (not Rosy Red) and so on.

Binders

Oil binders: Some of the popular binders found in oil paints are linseed oil or alkali refined linseed oil, poppy oil, sunflower oil, safflower oil. Old Holland uses cold-pressed extra virgin linseed oil.

Acrylic binders: Pigment is suspended in a 100% pure acrylic polymer emulsion binder. Retarders to slow down the drying time for acrylics are generally glycol or glycerin-based additives.

Watercolor binders: Arabic gum is used as the binder for watercolor. Additives may also be used such as glycerin, ox gall, honey used as preservatives. They may also help to alter the viscosity and help with the durability of a color.

Water mixable oil color binders: alkali-refined linseed oil, sunflower oils, or vegetable oils.

Cadmium

Cadmium Red is a known human carcinogen. It is extremely toxic if inhaled and slightly toxic if ingested but if used properly, poses no real threat. As a precaution, do not bring food near your paints or put brushes in your mouth to use as a holder. This could transfer traces of Cadmium into your body.

Color Code (Manufacturers Inventory Code)

This is the manufacturers' inventory code number that is given to each of the colors. This is primarily for ease of reference for retail and catalogue purposes and to aid you in buying your materials. This number is not usually listed on the tube.

Color Index Name (C.I. Name)

Each pigment can be universally identified by its Color Index Name, followed by a number referring to a standard list of pigments within each color category. This number is assigned as a pigment, is introduced for commercial use, and may be withdrawn or removed if the pigment is no longer manufactured. The symbol "N/A" for "not applicable" is used in the rare cases when a pigment is commercially available but is not included in the pigment list to protect a proprietary formulation.

The letter P denotes a pigment (rather than a dye, D, or a basic dye, B). You will occasionally see N which refers to natural pigments, such as cochineal, rose madder, gamboge, or lapis lazuli.

A letter to denote one of the ten basic color groups are as follows: Red=PR, Orange=PO, Yellow=PY, Green=PG, Blue=PB, Violet=PV, Brown=PBr, White=PW, Black=PBk and Metallic=PM.

An example of a color index name would be Cadmium Orange PO20.

A comprehensive pigment color chart may be found on http://www.artiscreation.com/

Color Index Number (C.I. No.)

The Color Index International is the standard compiled and published by both the Society of Dyers and Colorists, and the American Association of Textile Chemists and Colorists. The Color Index classifies pigments by their chemical composition. This information will allow you to research a specific pigment's working characteristics in reference books if you wish. The individual pigment is identified as usually a 5-digit number and may include more than one number. The composition of Cadmium Red is C.I. #77202 & #77196.

Of the two methods of reference, which being the Color Index Name and the Color Index Number, the former is most commonly used. In any case, the color index number or constitution number is the most reliable way to identify paint ingredients.

Chemical Description

The chemical description of the pigments is often useful for conservators. The color index name and number refer primarily to the chemical composition of the pigment. Color variation within the same CI name are produced through adjustments in the manufacturing methods (especially in the amount of time the pigment is calcinated and in the extent or method of grinding into fine particles), or through variations in the proportions of pigment ingredients or in the structure of the pigment crystal. Thus, the iron oxide color variations are produced by differences in the amount of added manganese, in the length of the calcination, and in the particle size. The cobalt and cadmium variations are produced by the particle sizes and the proportion of added secondary metals (tin or aluminum for cobalt's, selenium for cadmiums). The quinacridone variations are produced by the crystal form and particle size, and so on.

Granulating/Staining (ST) (Applies to Watercolor only)

In watercolor, some colors show a tendency to granulate and are marked as 'G'. Many artists use granulation to add visual texture to their paintings. As a general statement for watercolor, the traditional pigments that granulate are cobalt, earth colors, and ultramarines. The modern organic pigments like Phthalocyanine and Quinacridone do not granulate. In watercolor, these pigments are made of very fine particles which cause them to stain the paper. These colors are difficult to lift out completely. The traditional colors tend to lift from the paper more easily. If you wish to avoid granulation in your watercolor painting, the use of distilled water can reduce it in very hard water areas. Those colors not marked 'G' will tend to give a more uniform wash.

Visit http://www.handprint.com/HP/WCL/water.html which offers a wealth of information on watercolor pigments.

Health Labeling for the USA

Here is a brief outline of the labeling information that you can expect to find on artists' colors in the USA. The U.S. system labels all products whether a health warning is needed or not. The most common U.S. labels are: Approved Product "AP", and this indicates that the product has been tested by an independent toxicologist and is considered to be non-toxic. In the U.S., if a potential risk exists with a product, the label will say so. The Cautionary Label "CL" seal (replaced the Health Label "HL" seal in 2000) is used for products which are potentially hazardous, with proper phrases. For example, some cobalt colors may be labeled with this warning: "Warning: May produce allergic reaction by skin contact. Contains cobalt. Avoid skin contact. Wash hands after use. Keep out of reach of children".

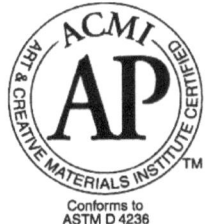 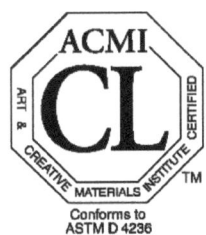

This specification establishes requirements for composition, physical properties, performance, and labeling of artists' oil, resin-oil, and alkyd paints. It also covers pigments, vehicles, and additives. Requirements are included for pigment identification, lightfastness, consistency, and drying time. The different labeling requirements for artists' oil paints, resin-oil, and alkyd paints are presented in detail, found at ASTM D4302—05(2010) for standards.

The labeling system came about through the combined efforts of a number of associations and groups. The American Society for Testing and Materials (ASTM) has prepared standards for the safe use of artists' materials. These have been published in a booklet entitled, "ASTM Standards for the Performance, Quality, and Health Labeling of Artists' Paints and Related Materials" (ISBN 0-8031-1838-4).

The labeling standard for Chronic Health Hazards in Art materials (ASTM D-4236) was codified into US law as part of the Federal Hazardous Substances Act. The Art & Creative Materials Institute (ACMI) provides labeling certification and works to promote the safe and informed use of art materials in North America.

From the year 2000, many art materials sold in the United States have included added labeling for products containing cadmium and lead as a result of action surrounding California's Safe Drinking Water and Toxic Enforcement Act of 1986 (commonly known as Proposition 65). The new labels will reflect requirements resulting from Proposition 65, independent of labeling required by the Federal Hazardous Substances Act.

For example, the labels for cadmium-containing products will read:

"DO NOT SPRAY APPLY. This product contains cadmium, a chemical known to the State of California to cause cancer by means of inhalation."

Note: There is no direct relationship between the EU (European Union) and USA systems of health labeling as the categories used have different levels and limits, e.g., flammable in the USA is not automatically considered as flammable in the EU.

Lake Pigments

A lake pigment is a pigment created by a manufacturer by mixing a powdered dye color with an inert binder usually a metallic salt. Rose madder is an example of a lake pigment; the color comes from a dye created from madder root. The madder root is ground down to form the dye substance. Manufacturers and suppliers to artists and industry often omit the lake designation in the name. Many lake pigments are fugitive because the dyes involved are unstable when exposed to light.

Lightfastness or Permanence Rating

The ASTM (American Society for Testing & Materials) sets the standards for the performance of art materials including a color's lightfastness. To measure lightfastness using this system, colors are reduced to a level of 40% reflectance by the addition of Titanium White, (except for watercolor which relies on the white paper). This means the amount of light reflected from the color swatch. The swatches are then tested in both sunlight and artificially accelerated conditions. Coloring materials tested with this method receive a Lightfastness Rating. The ASTM appoints a roman numeral for the lightfastness (I, II, III, IV, or V), but you may find that some Manufacturers label theirs with a number. Only Lightfastness Ratings of I and II are considered permanent for artists use. The permanence of an artists' color is defined as "its durability when laid with a brush on paper or canvas, graded appropriately and displayed under a glass frame in a dry room freely exposed to ordinary daylight and an ordinary town atmosphere". This definition reflects the manner in which one expects to find paintings displayed.

When multiple pigments are used to produce a new color, the manufacturer will show that all the colors used produces a Permanent color, indicating this by using the word *Permanent* in the colors marked as Permanent Alizarin Crimson (made with PR122 Quinacridone Red).

I   *Extremely Permanent

I   Excellent

II   Good

III   Moderate

IV   Poor

V   Fugitive - Pigments that are not permanent are called fugitives. Fugitive pigments fade over time, or with exposure to light, while some eventually blacken. Some fugitive colors may exist in student grade paints and are ok for studies and temporary artworks.

For further information on some colors, the rating may include one or more of the following additions:

(i)   *'A' rated in full strength may fade in thin washes

(ii)   **Cannot be relied upon to withstand damp

(iii)   ***Bleached by acids, acidic atmospheres

(iv)   ***Fluctuating color; fades in light, recovers in dark

(v)   ****Should not be prepared in pale tints with Flake White, as these will fade

(vi)   'A' rated with a coating of fixative

Where no ASTM rating is given for a color, it is denoted as N/L meaning "Not Listed". This usually indicates that the pigment or the type of range has not yet been tested by the ASTM. It does not necessarily indicate a lack of lightfastness.

Manufacturers Grade of Paints

Generally speaking, the student grade paints are blends of pigments which are less expensive for the manufacturers to use, or the tubes of paint may contain less of the color pigment itself and be diluted with more binder. This can produce a very weak version of the color you are trying to mix. My philosophy is to buy the best paint you can afford and above all choose the colors that contain only one pure pigment. You do not have to replace your colors at this time but consider replacing your student grade colors for the better quality over time.

Some paint color manufacturers offer two or three levels of quality for their product. The quality is based on the ratio of how much of the color pigment is used, the type of pigment (organic vs. synthetic), how finely ground the pigment is and how much binder they use in the recipe. For student or non-permanent grade paint, the manufacturer will generally use the inexpensive color substitutes, fugitive colors or mix a blend of synthetic with organic color pigments to reduce costs.

Be sure you know the quality of your paint. Student grades may have non-permanent pigments as well as less pigment and more of the binder making it more difficult to obtain good coverage. The good news for painters is that many of the fugitive, non-permanent as well as toxic pigments have been replaced now in most paints, both artist and scholastic, and are reasonably priced. If you wish to produce a work of art, you will need to ask yourself if it is worthy of permanent pigments?

Artists' grade refers to the highest quality paint.

Student grade refers to use for students for temporary or non-permanent use.

Scholastic refers to grade school use and non-permanent.

Opaque Color

Opaque colors are marked on tube as 'O' and semi-opaque are marked as 'SO'. Opaque colors are typically dense and heavy in weight. Their pigments have clays, heavy metals, iron, or all of the above. Examples of opaque pigments are any of the Cadmium colors & Titanium White. These colors will often dominate other colors when mixing so knowing which are transparent and which are opaque are important factors when mixing. Cadmium Red PR108 has a far greater tinting strength than the transparent color of Hansa Yellow PY3. To mix the color orange as an example, start with Lemon Yellow PY3 (a transparent color) and add a very small amount of Cadmium Red (an opaque color) into it. This ratio might be something like 10:1; ten parts Yellow to one-part Red. If you start the other way around, with red and add the yellow, you will find yourself with more orange than you will need.

Organic vs Inorganic

Organic Pigments
Of natural origin, animal, or vegetable (Living).
Usually Carbon Compounds.

Animal

- Caput Mortuum or Mummy brown (from the ground up remains of Egyptian mummies)
- Carmine (kermesic acid from the cochineal insect)
- Indian Yellow (from the urine of cows that are fed mango leaves)
- Sepia (cuttlefish ink)

Vegetable

- Madder (from the root of the common madder plant)
- Gamboge (from the gum resin of the Garcinia tree in Thailand)
- Indigo (from plants cultivated in India)

Inorganic Pigments
Chemical compounds from chemical elements other than carbons (Non-Living)

Earth Pigments

- Green Earth (a clay that is colored by small amounts of iron and manganese)

- Ochre (derived from naturally tinted clay having mineral oxides)

- Sienna (earth mined from Siena, Italy)

- Umber (earth mined from Umbria, Italy)

- Venetian Red (originally native earth having 15 to 40 percent iron oxide)

Mineral Pigments

- Lapis Lazuli (semi-precious stone has been used for over 6,000 years and found primarily in Badakhshan, a province of Afghanistan)

- Malachite Blue (basic carbonate of copper)

- Vermillion (cinnabar was used by China at an early date and up to the eighth century)

Synthetic Inorganic Pigments
Do not occur in nature but are artificial and manufactured as Carbons, Metallic or Minerals.

- Cadmiums
- Cerulean Blue (a compound of cobalt and tin oxides)
- Prussian Blue (Ferric-ferrocyanide, originally meaning "blue compound of iron")
- Zinc Oxide (used for Zinc White)

Synthetic Organic Pigments
Complex carbon compounds which do not occur in nature but are created in the laboratory.

- Azo Pigments (Yellow to Red)
- Dioxazine (Violet).
- Isoindolinones
- Phthalocyanine (Blues and Greens)
- Quinacridones (Red-Violets)

Semi-Transparent Color

Semi-transparent 'ST' colors have a little more tinting strength than a Transparent Color. A translucent color allows some transparency.

Series Number

The Series Number of a color is set by the manufacturer and indicates the relative price of the color determined by the cost of the raw pigment. Series 1 is the least expensive and Series 6 the most expensive.

Tinting Strength

When a color is mixed with White it is labeled as a tint. This will help you decide how strong or weak the color is when mixed with other colors.

Translucent Color

Light passes through translucent color but it is diffused, and these pigments can be less intense. Frosted" glass would be a good description of translucent light.

Transparent Color

Transparent colors are marked on tube as 'T'. A transparent color offers a weak tinting strength when mixed with more opaque colors, but it has uses in glazes. Transparent colors allow the under color (or white of paper or canvas) to show through. Transparent colors typically come from colored liquids such as dyes. Examples of transparent colors are Quinacridone Red PR122, Phthalo Blue PB15, Phthalo Green PG36 and Lemon Yellow PY3.

Transparency can vary from one manufacturer to another, so the ratings are provided as a general guide only. In addition, any color can be made more transparent by adding a medium to it creating a film of color that will appear more transparent than would normally be found out of the tube.

Toxicity Labeling

Health labeling on your paint tube is described as follows:

The hazardous property is a general designation of a possible hazard. It is assumed intelligent people will use at least ordinary care when handling all paints or pigments. The designation has been arrived at, in most cases, by the manufacturer's literature, MSDS sheets at the Oxford University Chemical Laboratory, or the City of Tucson's Environmental Management Division's searchable database of Health & Safety in the Arts. All paints and especially dry pigments can be hazardous if carelessly handled, but if handled properly with common sense all but the most dangerous can be used safely.

A = Low hazard, but do not handle carelessly.

B = Possible Hazard if improperly or carelessly handled.

C = Hazardous, use proper precautions for handling mildly toxic substances.

D = Extremely Toxic, only attempt working with this pigment (especially the dry form) in laboratory like conditions and with proper safety equipment. See "Prudent practices in the laboratory: handling and disposal of chemicals" for more info.

Identify your Colors

Now it's your turn to get your paints out and identify the bias of your own tube colors. Set your Color Wheel on a table and place the tube colors in a circle. For dark colors, you may need to open the tube of color and swipe the open end on a white piece of paper to better name its bias.

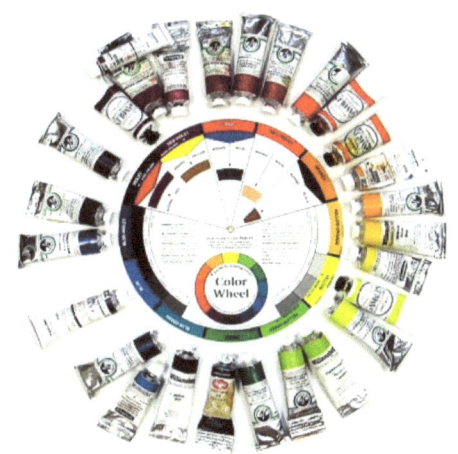

Create an Inventory of your Colors

Now that you have sorted your colors, you can begin inventorying your tube colors. You can use a piece of 81/2" x 11" card stock to make a chart similar to the illustration to the right.

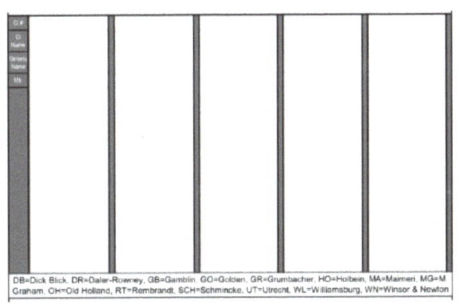

With each tube in hand, record the Color Index # (PR108) Color Index Name (Cadmium Red Medium), the Generic Tube Color Name (Manufacturer's color name), the Manufacturer's name (abbreviated i.e., Winsor & Newton would be WN). You can also record the Lightfastness or Permanence rating (I-V), and whether it is a Transparent or Opaque (T or O) color in on the Mfg line. If you have paint tubes older than the year 2000, this information may not be available on the tube, but you may be able to find it online at Dick Blick Art Materials if the manufacturer is still producing the color. I have found this to be a good source for all the technical stuff.

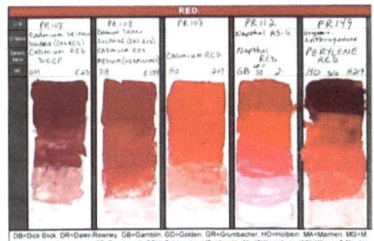
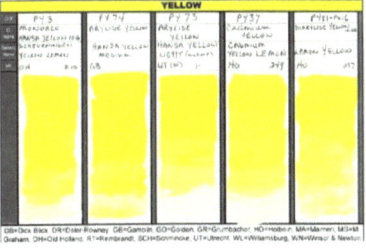
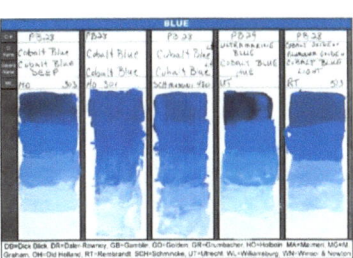

Use a palette knife to smear a small amount of each color under the appropriate color names. Look for single pigment colors as they will produce the best color mixes. Add white to reveal the different value ranges of these colors.

Colors found in tubes under any given color name, are not absolute and variations may be vast from one manufacturer to another. Use your own favorite colors to start with. You can experiment with new colors as you fully understand the bias of the ones you have. These choices are all subjective and there are many variables in choosing colors for any painting. None will be considered a right or wrong choice. Go with what you like.

If you are missing any of the colors represented on the Color Wheel, you may want to add it to your inventory to have on hand. You can always mix a batch of that missing color. Over time you can build the inventory of the basic twelve colors.

If you buy a tube color you do not like, you may have to live with it or give it to a friend who can use it. In either case, record it so you will have a record of the color and it will serve as a reminder that you do not want to make the same mistake again. These words are spoken from experience.

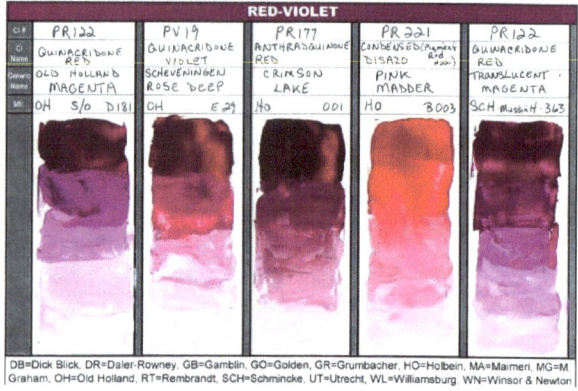

You may own more than one color tube for each group on the wheel: for instance, RED-VIOLET. You may have Permanent Alizarin Crimson and Magenta among other color names. There are many other colors that fall into RED-VIOLET category. I will address how to select the best color for a specific Color Scheme later.

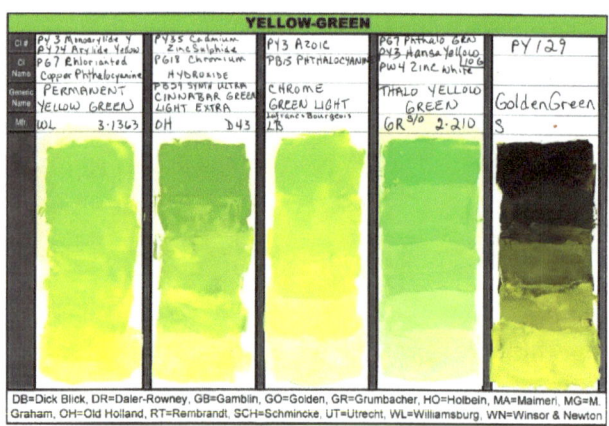

YELLOW-GREEN tends to be the most difficult color to find with enough yellow bias. If you cannot find a hue with enough Yellow bias, you may want to mix your own. You can pre-mix a large amount of the color and store into an empty aluminum paint tubes bought at online art supply retailers.

You will start distinguishing color bias as you begin creating your own color chart inventory. Some colors may have a use in multiple color categories, i.e. Cadmium Yellow Medium or Deep could be used as YELLOW-ORANGE and Cadmium Yellow Light may be used as YELLOW-ORANGE and YELLOW. You may record these dual use colors in multiple places on your inventory cards.

Record your Browns, Earth, and Neutral colors the same way as your basic 12 colors. After you record them though, I recommend placing these tubes in a container and out of sight for just a little while so you will not be tempted to use them and just until you get more comfortable with this controlled color scheme approach.

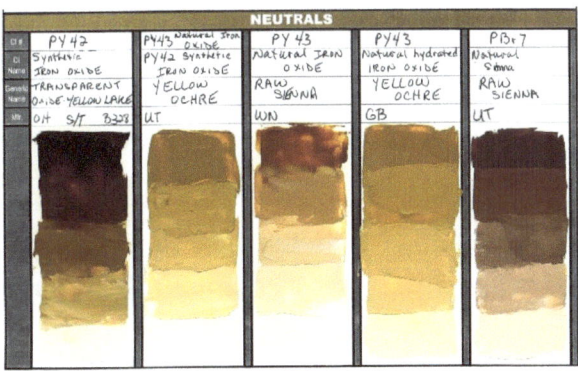

I consider most of the neutrals like Yellow Ochre to be convenience colors that will usually be modified by the artist in the painting process. There is not much of an advantage over mixing the color yourself using pure pigment. Premixed paints can hide flaws in the quality of the paint, while mixing a neutral color using the colors in your scheme will be more predictable.

You may record Black and White tube colors. I do not use Black on my palette as I prefer to mix chromatic darks as I prefer to call them, mixing colors from within the color scheme I've chosen. Black can be useful to create interesting greens, however.

There is no better way to understand Color Mixing than to record your own color swatches. It is the best method of finding the true color bias in your tubes. You cannot rely on the colors printed from books as these are printers' ink and will not match your tube color. There is nothing like the real thing!

Detailed information on tube color pigments can be found at the Dick Blick website under each manufacturer. Another helpful website for pigment identification is Artiscreation.com. Additional websites are found in the Reference section of this book.

Chapter 4
COLOR SCHEMES
DEFINED, ILLUSTRATED AND CHOOSING

A controlled palette refers to the use of colors that are planned and limited in an effort to create a harmonious piece of artwork. When you use colors in a defined combination such as Analogous, Complementary, Triad or Tetrad this is referred to as a color scheme. These schemes are the key to creating a harmonious painting.

The following are some common color schemes defined and illustrated. By changing color bias in any of these schemes the variations are endless. This is just the beginning of what is possible.

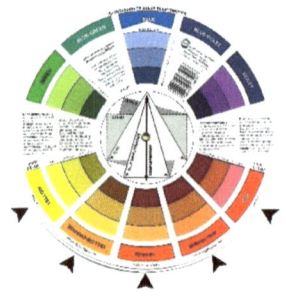 **ANALOGOUS** uses any shade, tint or tone of colors that lie next to each other on the wheel. When using this color scheme be sure that one of these colors is dominant. The Analogous color scheme can include three to five consecutive colors as illustrated in the diagram.

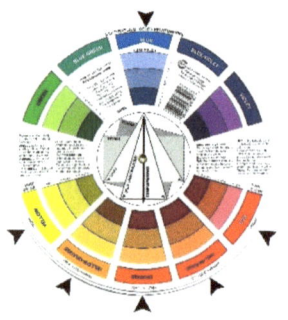 **ANALOGOUS-COMPLEMENTARY**: Four to six colors make up this color scheme. The dominant color (ORANGE) and the Complementary plus two to four, adjacent colors to the dominant color, make up the color scheme.

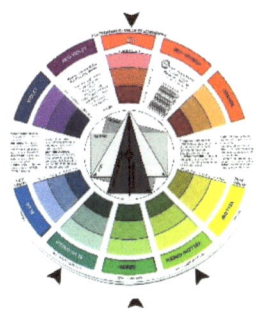

COMPLEMENTARY: Harmonious color combinations can be produced using any two colors opposite each other on the Color Wheel such as RED/GREEN. These are called Complementary colors. Other pairs of Complementary colors may include ORANGE/BLUE and YELLOW/VIOLET. Mixing a set of Complementary colors will produce a neutral color with a bias toward one of the contributing colors.

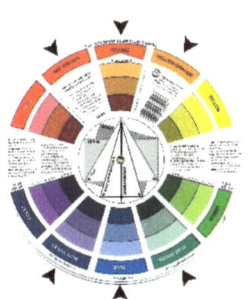

When using the Complementary color scheme, you may want to expand the use of colors to include the warm and cool of each Complementary color as shown in the diagram. Complementary schemes can also be chosen using pairs of Tertiary colors as well. Complementary schemes can also be chosen using all the Tertiary colors as shown as a Split Primary.

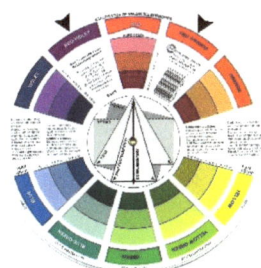

DIAD: Just as the name implies, di meaning two; this color scheme uses two colors that are two color steps apart on the Color Wheel.

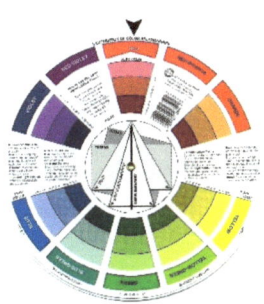

MONO-CHROMATIC: Any one color plus black and white using varying shades, tints, or tones. RED, WHITE, and BLACK make a mono-chromatic color scheme. Being the simplest of schemes, it allows for value checks in a painting without the need to focus on multiple colors.

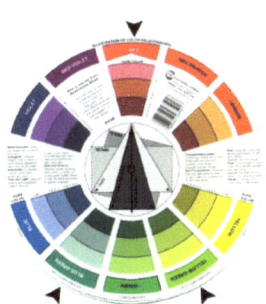

SPLIT COMPLEMENTARY: The top of the isosceles triangle stands for the dominant color for your artwork. The two split Complementary colors will be shown at the bottom corners of the isosceles triangle. In this example, RED is the main color with BLUE-GREEN and YELLOW-GREEN, as the other contributing split Complementary colors. There are twelve Split-Complementary Color Schemes.

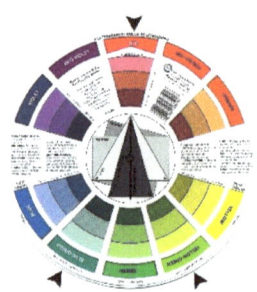

SPLIT PRIMARY: This scheme excludes the primary and secondary colors. It uses all the tertiary colors. It could also be considered the warm and cool bias of each primary, conveniently spaced as every other color around the Color Wheel. These names are RED-VIOLET, RED-ORANGE, YELLOW-ORANGE, YELLOW-GREEN, BLUE-GREEN, and BLUE-VIOLET.

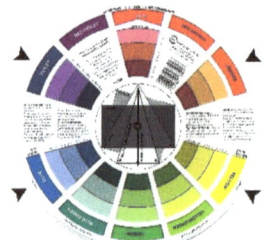

TETRAD (rectangle): Any four colors forming a rectangle which equates to two pairs of Complementary colors. The complementary pairs illustrated to the left are VIOLET/YELLOW and BLUE/ORANGE.

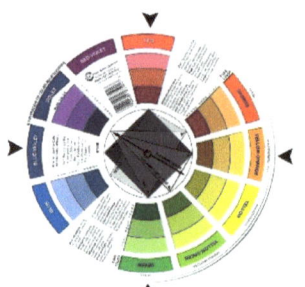

TETRAD (square): Any four colors forming a geometric square equating to two pairs of Complementary colors. The complementary pairs illustrated to the left are RED/GREEN and BLUE VIOLET/YELLOW ORANGE.

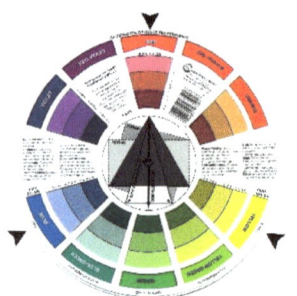

TRIAD: A traditional Triad is any three colors symmetrically spaced around the Color Wheel forming a triangle called a Triad representing RED YELLOW and BLUE as shown in the illustration below.

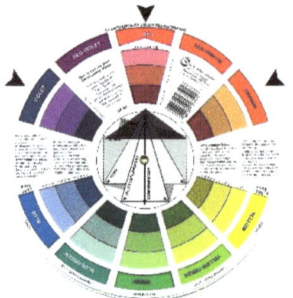

Another type of Triad color scheme may be modified to a near analogous color scheme as illustrated to the left. This scheme skips only one color in between.

Identify the Dominant Color

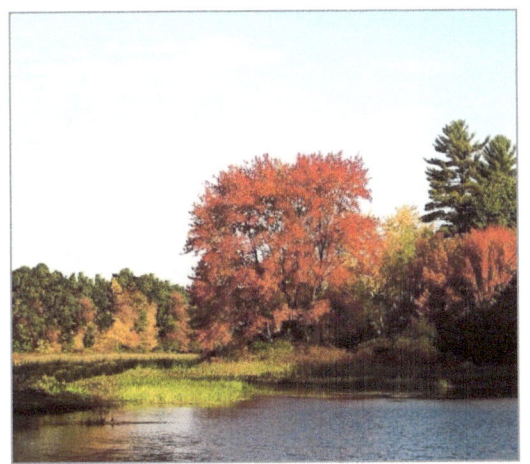

A dominant color is that which takes the most physical space in a picture. Choosing the best Color Scheme for your painting requires that you determine the dominant color of your subject, before choosing the other contributing colors. While the dominant color may be obvious in some paintings, examining the bias of the contributing colors in your subject will lead you to the determination of the best color scheme. Some subjects may be difficult to find a dominant color, but the fact remains that there needs to be one.

Using the reference photo above, let's say blue is the dominant color. The question is which blue best describes the Blue you want to use? Is it BLUE-GREEN (Phthalo Blue PB15:3), BLUE (Cobalt Blue PB28) or BLUE-VIOLET (Ultramarine Blue PB29). Reading this book in print, or as an e-version, might display a different blue bias in each case, but for the sake of simplifying, we will choose BLUE (Cobalt Blue PB28) as the dominant blue.

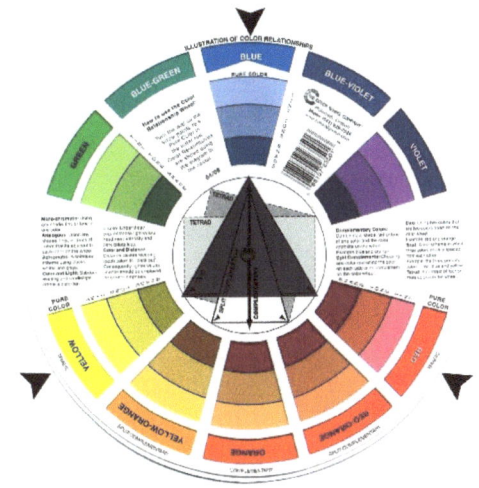

TRIAD Color Scheme

Start with the simplest color scheme, a Triad of primary colors, which offers the purest of possible colors. With BLUE at the top of the wheel, place the equilateral triangle, arrow side up toward BLUE. The other two corners that make up the Triad, point to RED and YELLOW. To paint the picture below I used Cobalt Blue PB28, Cadmium Red Medium PR108 and Hansa Yellow PY3.

Paint a practice color card mixing as shown in the illustration, the Triad of colors to produce a variety of oranges, greens and violets. By adding small amounts of white toward the center of the color card, the intensity of each color will change. In the center are a few complementary mixes to create neutrals.

67

Can you identify all the colors on the painted color card that are seen in the painting?

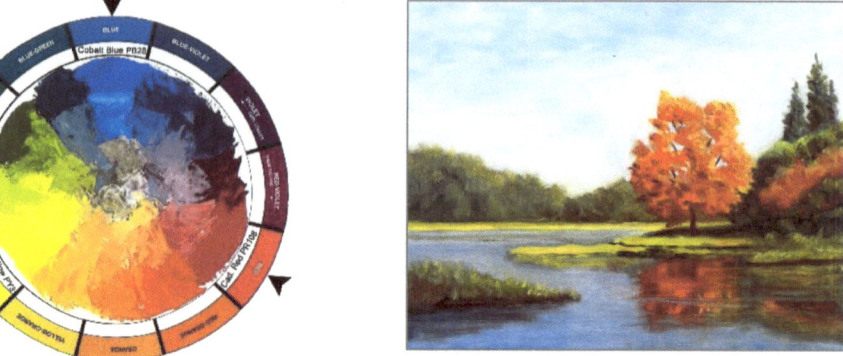

Kendall Pond, *8"x10" oil,* Triad color scheme

Each practice color card you produce may look different depending on the tube colors you choose. The goal is to see if you can achieve all the colors you need for your painting before you start painting. Remember that you are not trying to color match your photograph because inks produce a different color than paint pigment.

These exercises serve as a trial run for the color scheme you will use throughout your painting. The more you experiment with color variations in a Triad, the more you will become in tune with color bias. Also keep in mind the opaqueness or transparency of each pigment.

There is no right or wrong color scheme, just the one you envision for your own painting.

TRIAD with a different dominant Blue

Not happy with the outcome of your first Color Scheme? Try adjusting the dominant blue color with a BLUE-GREEN or BLUE-VIOLET instead. There are no rules saying that you cannot change what Mother Nature, or your reference photo is showing you. Feel free to change your dominant Blue to one that is more pleasing to you or suits your needs better. Here are two more examples of a Triad scheme using a different dominant BLUE. Notice the wide variety of colors that each scheme produces.

BLUE-GREEN   **BLUE-VIOLET**

TETRAD with the original BLUE

You may find that the Triadic color scheme limits your desired colors, so when this happens feel free to explore other Color Schemes. Consider expanding to a Tetrad which uses a double set of Complementary colors, four colors total. You can use the original dominant BLUE or try a BLUE-GREEN or BLUE-VIOLET as the dominant color instead. In this painting illustration, I chose the original BLUE as Cobalt Blue PB28 for the dominant color. The other contributing colors are ORANGE as Cadmium Orange PO20, RED-VIOLET as Permanent Alizarin Crimson PR122 and YELLOW-GREEN as a Permanent Yellow Green (various mix).

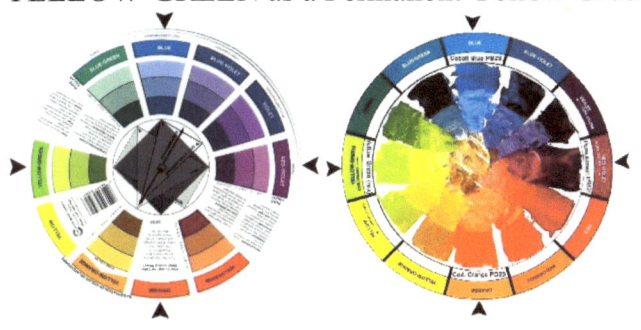
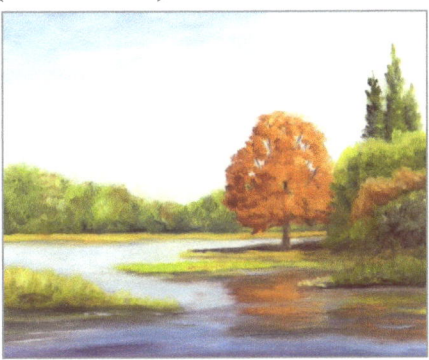

Kendall Pond. *8"x10" oil.* Tetrad color scheme

COMPLEMENTARY Color Scheme

Let's consider one more variation while we are reviewing how to get to your color palette choice. This example uses a Complementary color scheme with the original dominant BLUE as Cobalt Blue PB28 and Complementary color ORANGE as Cadmium Orange PO20. In this example I chose to expand the color range of this color scheme by adding the warm and cool of each color. The extended Blue palette would be BLUE-VIOLET as Ultramarine Blue PB29 (warm) and BLUE-GREEN as Phthalo Blue PB15 (cool). The extended Orange palette would be YELLOW-ORANGE as Cadmium Yellow Medium PY35 (warm) and RED-ORANGE as Cadmium Red Light PR108 (cool).

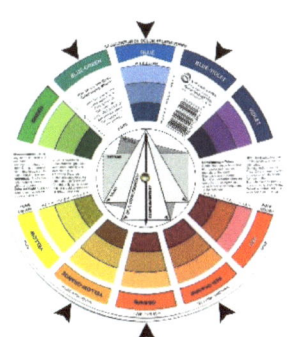
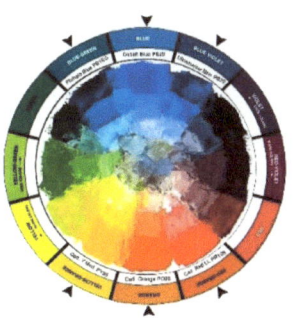

Kendall Pond, *8"x10" oil*
Complementary color scheme

Identify the Dominant Color of a Neutral

Identifying the dominant color for a predominantly neutral painting can be challenging. With subjects such as rocks or sand, you will need to look past the neutral color and find the subtle underlying color. Gray and Brown are not one of the twelve color groups on the wheel, so you need to choose the color you feel best represents one of those colors. Refer to the list of Brown, Earth, and Neutral colors in Chapter 2, pg. 48 to help you choose. Paint a practice color card using any of the color schemes with the Brown, Earth and Neutral colors or mix them using pure traditional colors.

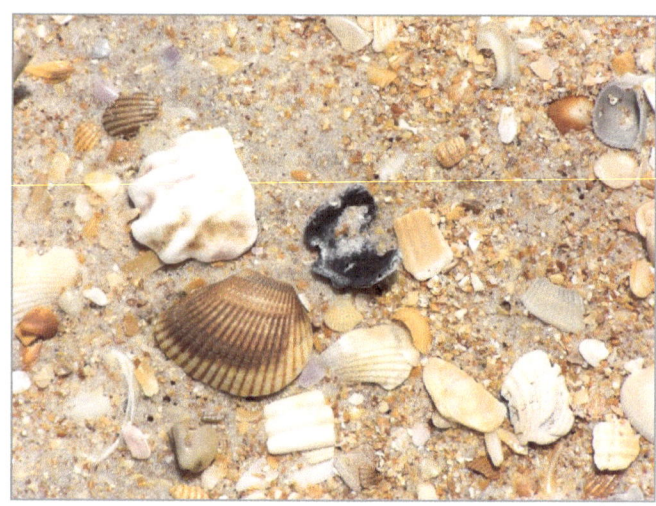

In the shell photo, the dominant color might be ORANGE. It does not have to be an exact match to your photo reference.

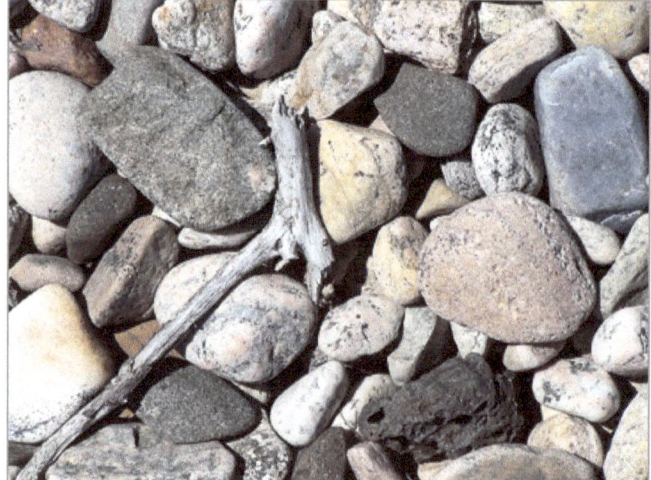

In the photo of the rocks to the left, the dominant color might be BLUE-VIOLET, VIOLET or possibly RED-VIOLET.

Change the Composition to Create Dominance

Sometimes the dominant color in a photo reference is split equally in half by two colors as the photo (left picture) below illustrates. In this case, you will first need to choose which area will be dominant in the composition, sky, or sand?

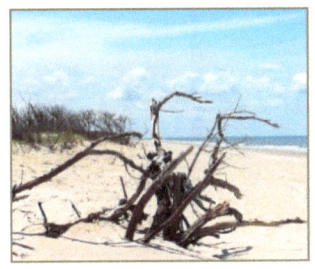
Equal dominance

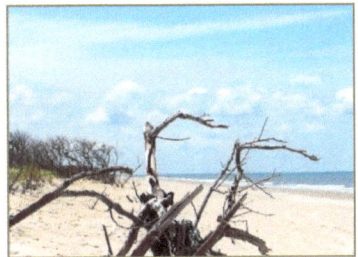
Sky is dominant

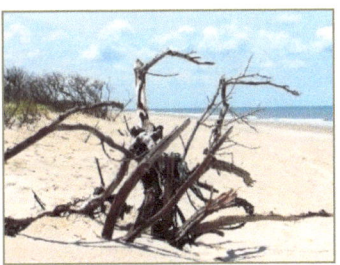
Sand is dominant

If you would want the sky to be the dominant area, the composition needs to reflect this so the horizon line is lowered as shown in the middle photo above. This now creates a BLUE dominance.

If the sand is to be the dominant area, the horizon line is moved up as shown in the right photo above. Although one may be perplexed as to what *color* sand may be, it can often be identified as an ORANGE. When ORANGE is neutralized with the complementary color, BLUE, you will create a sand color, adjusting and adding White, as necessary.

Record your Color Schemes

Record your color schemes on blank card stock, canvas paper, watercolor paper, or illustration board. Whichever surface you chose, I recommended making them 8 ½" x 11" so they can be stored in a notebook for quick reference at a later date. A free template is also available to print at WhiteBirchFineArt.com under Classes section.

A small palette knife makes applying the color mixes go quickly. Make notes of the combinations or recipes directly on the sheets. Abbreviate your notes to read something like this: 3Y:1BG which translates to three parts YELLOW to one-part BLUE-GREEN.

• Write your color scheme at the top.

• Make notes about the tube colors, i.e. this Orange color has a strong Yellow bias.

• Label the tube color with as much information as you can. The manufacturer's color name, (Red Light), Color Index (CI) name (Cadmium Red Light PR108), and manufacturer's name (Winsor and Newton), Lightfastness (I-V) and Opacity if available.

• Mix colors with a little white to reveal the lighter versions as well as mixing a variety of neutrals or grays using the contributing Complementary colors in the scheme. You will be surprised how many color variations you can make with just a few colors!

• Mix color schemes systematically in a circle as represented in the Color Wheel below and in the illustrations throughout this book. You could also mix the colors for the scheme sparsely, creating only the colors you plan to use for now.

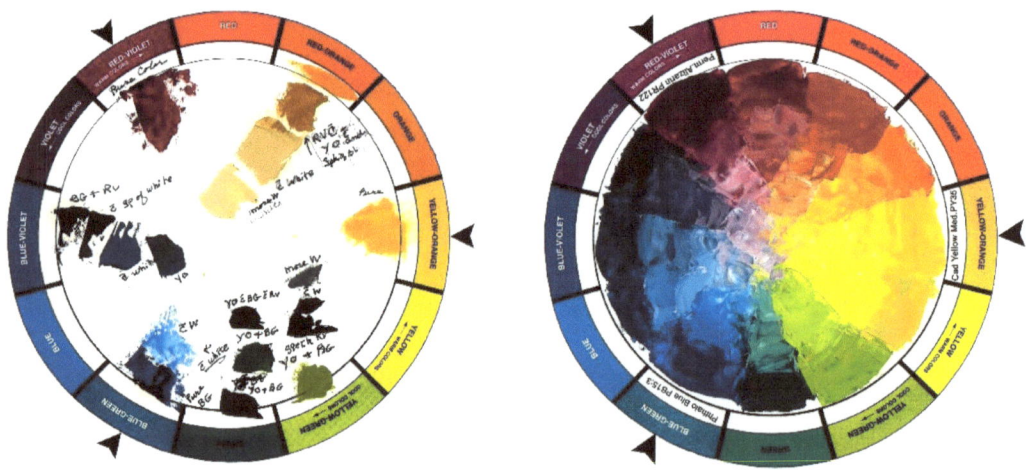

SUMMARY

New Habits

Work toward a new habit of taking the time to choose a color scheme based on the dominant color. Then on a color card paint samples of your colors before you start your painting. This will serve as a trial run and reference sheet for the color scheme you will use. It does not take much pre-painting time and is time well spent to ensure you have chosen the correct color scheme. It is far more frustrating to discover halfway through your painting that the colors you chose are not working for you.

My philosophy for adding other tube colors to any scheme is that, if you can mix the color using the contributing colors, then, you could add an additional tube color if you would like. But why not just mix the color instead of adding another tube of paint? Unless the color will be used extensively or the color is important to the outcome of the painting, I would suggest mixing the variations and watching the magic that happens!

Freedom to Play

Allow yourself the time and freedom to explore the different color schemes as well as new tube colors. I encourage you to stray from your regular tube colors to create new color schemes. Try choosing a brighter intensity color scheme using bright colors or maybe an all neutral one. You may find that you prefer using the Triad color scheme offering only three colors or you may like the Complementary color scheme expanding the palette to six colors. You may choose a different color scheme for the same reference photo as a friend and that is okay. We all have our own thought process and create differently. The combinations can sometimes feel endless but by practicing the different color schemes, you will soon find that they are worthwhile and become second nature to you.

Creating a Library

By applying this practice of recording each new color scheme on color cards, you will be creating a library of color schemes to be used as reference for future works. Keep these color cards accessible so the next time you choose the same color scheme, you can use them again by simply reviewing the color card and possibly adding to it for your next project. Soon you will have built a library of reference cards that you will use for a lifetime and choosing a color scheme will be a snap.

Chapter 5
Triad Color Schemes

The traditional Triad color scheme uses three (3) colors equally spaced around the Color Wheel. This is a popular scheme among artists because it offers strong visual contrast while keeping harmony and color richness. The Triadic color scheme is not as contrasting as the Complementary scheme, but it looks more balanced and harmonious. Using a group of traditional colors (primaries) for a Triad color scheme will be just the starting point in creating harmonious color schemes.

Primary colors in a TRIAD Color Scheme

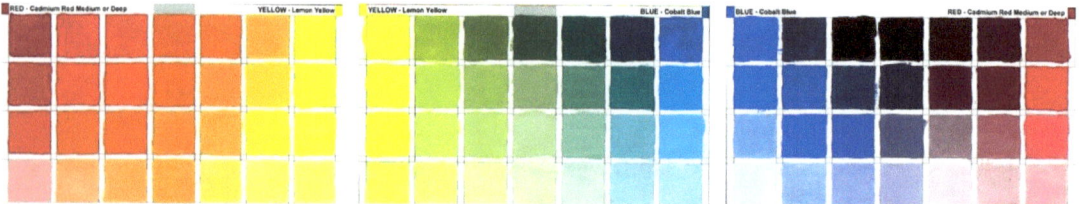

The chart directly below illustrates the range of secondary colors that can be mixed using the three primary colors. The top row is the pure color and the second thru fourth rows have the inclusion of white to tint or lighten the colors.

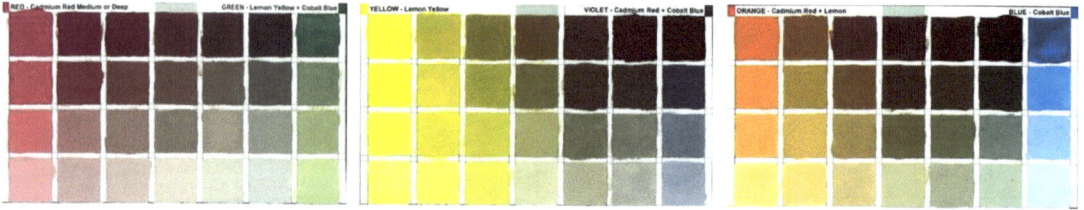

The chart below illustrates a range of secondary and neutral colors that can be mixed using a pure primary color (RED on the left) and a mix of two primary colors producing a secondary color (GREEN on the right). White was added in the second thru fourth rows to create lighter tints of the colors.

The primary Triad color scheme is the most basic scheme but can offer such a wide range of colors as the charts reveal. Practice this color scheme and see just how many colors are possible!

Primary colors in a TRIAD Color Scheme

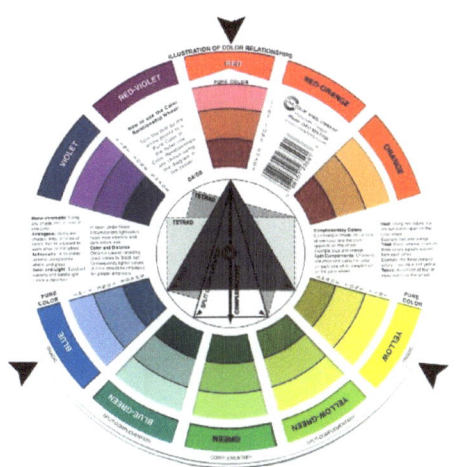 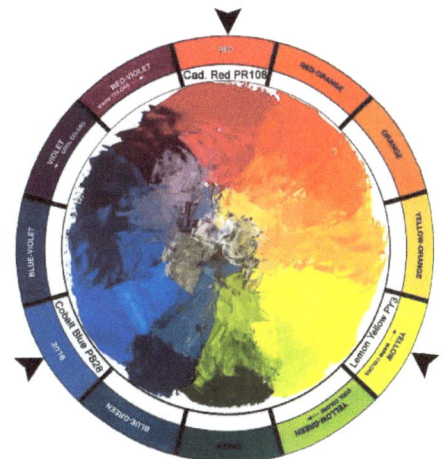

In this illustration, I used the Triad of Primary colors. The practice Color Wheel above reveals all the mixes of colors I can achieve with RED as Cadmium Red Medium PR108, YELLOW as Lemon Yellow PY3 and BLUE as Cobalt Blue PB28.

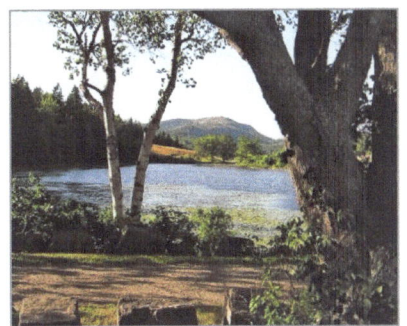

Photos and printers' inks do not register darks well. The photo reference, left, is quite dark and lacks the color, which attracted me to paint it, in the first place. More often than not, the dark areas in a photo appear to be nearly black as shown in the photo to the left. This does not mean that you should reach for your

black to darken colors or paint your subject in black. Try using Complementary colors to create chromatic darks. Use your reference as a means to capture your idea, not copy the colors in the photo exactly as you see it. Painting should be a free expression of your intent and only by using your reference more

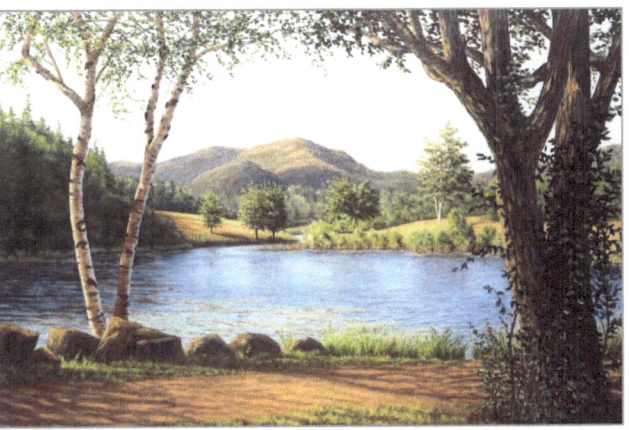

Mt. Bernard, Acadia National Park, *24"x36" oil*

loosely will you gain the freedom and not just a color matching process. Have the confidence to exaggerate the colors you see in your reference. This is what will make your paintings your own vision.

Secondary colors in a TRIAD Color Scheme

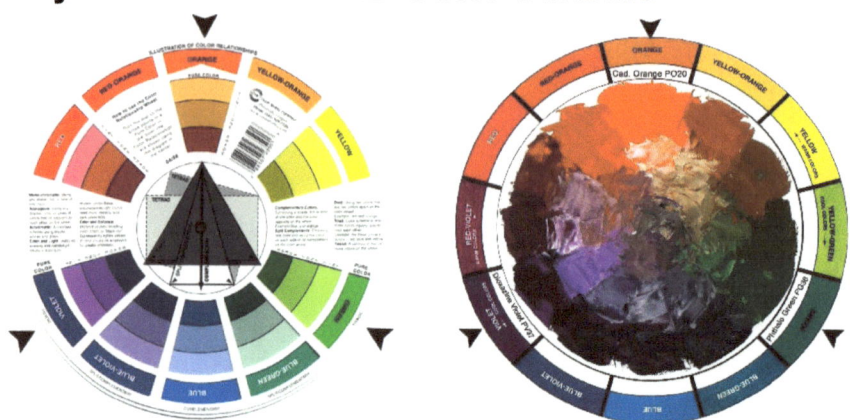

The Secondary Color Triad Scheme may be one of the most intriguing to use. You need to carefully select each color bias, asking yourself what the color needs to be. By creating multiple charts using differing biases you will be able to determine which is best for your work.

I found Italy to be especially well suited for this color palette. For *Tuscany Manor*, I used Cadmium Orange PO20, Chromium Oxide Green PG17, and Dioxazine Violet PV37. While I am not a big advocate of using green from a tube color, I did use Chromium Oxide Green PG17 for my green in this painting. I first created a close Chromium Oxide Green by mixing Permanent Green PG36 plus Cadmium Orange PO20. By knowing first that I can make the color with my selected pure colors, I am then confident that the harmonization of the painting will stay intact. While I much prefer to mix my own greens so I can achieve a wide range of variations, I altered Chromium Oxide Green as with any green, by mixing it with other colors on my palette. I never use any color straight out of the tube.

I used two reference photos for the painting *Tuscany Manor*. The left one was used for the lighting on the buildings and the right one was used for the foreground and composition.

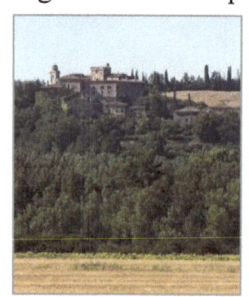

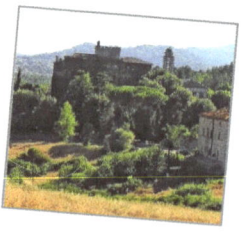

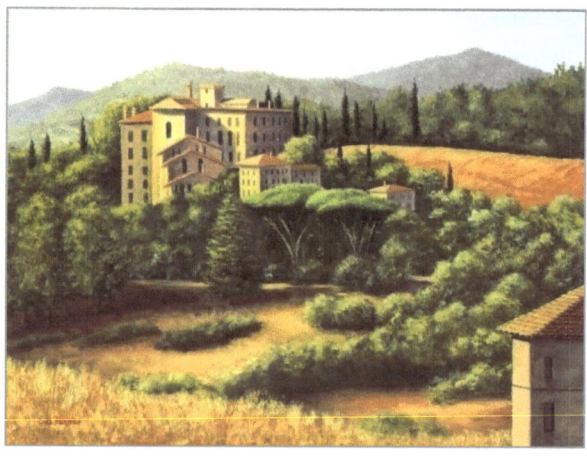

Tuscan Manor, *12"x16" oil, private collection*

76

Tertiary colors in a TRIAD Color Scheme I

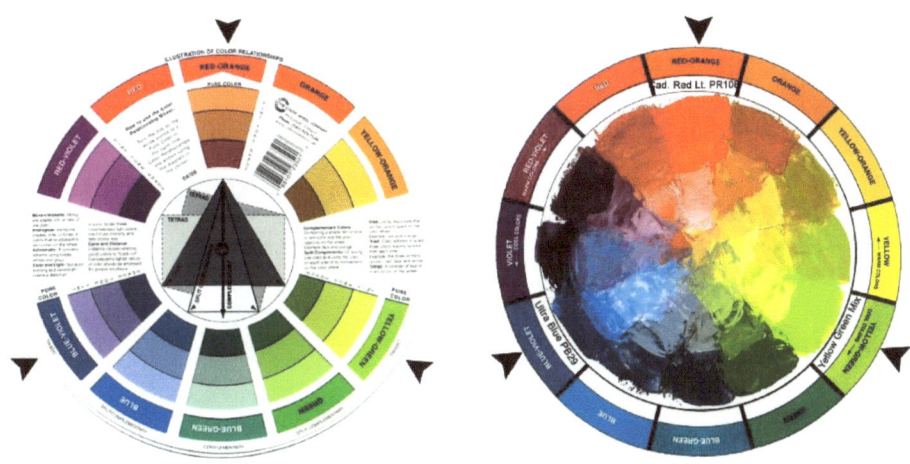

This Triad of colors produces lots of neutralized colors typically found in nature and works well for woodsy scenes.

The colors used in *Merging Lanes,* were Cadmium Red Medium PR108, Permanent Yellow Green (permanent mix) and Ultramarine Blue PB29.

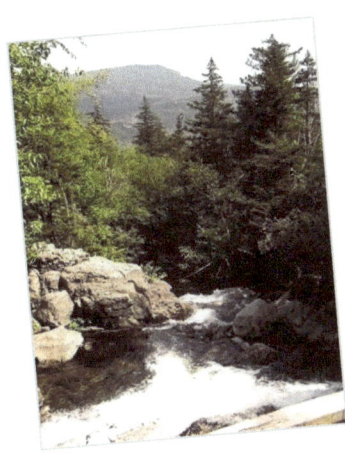

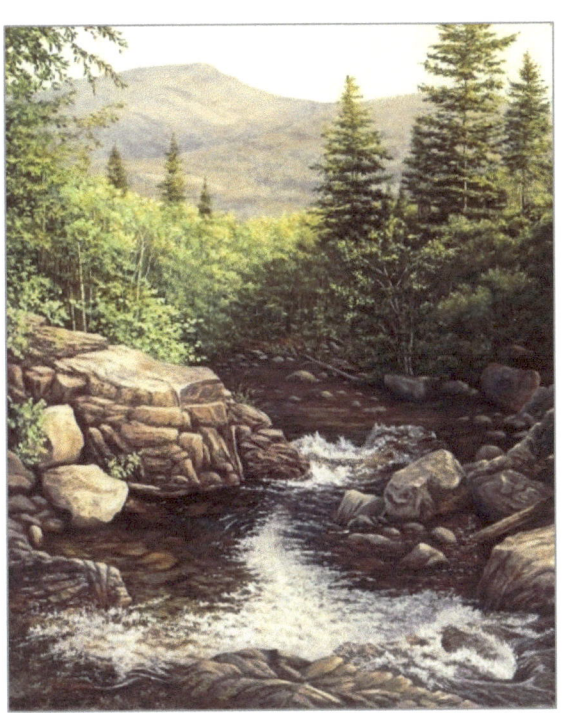

Merging Lanes, *30"x24" oil, private collection*

Tertiary colors in a TRIAD Color Scheme II

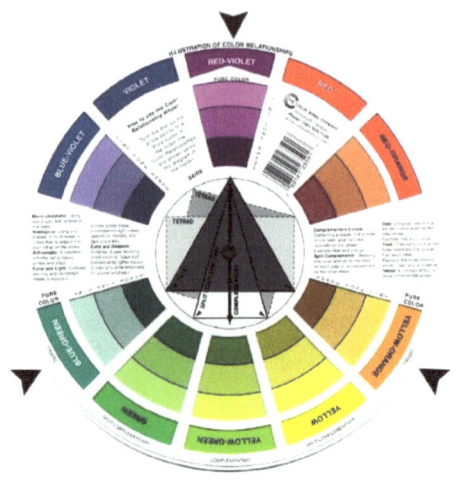 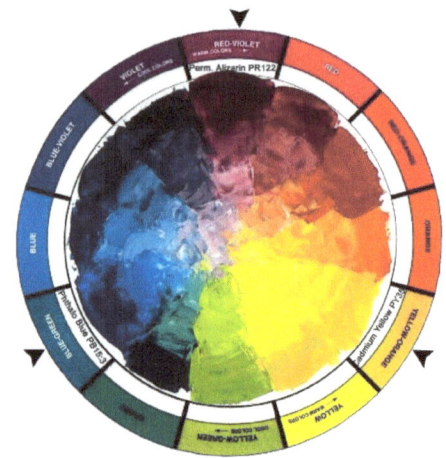

This scheme is similar to the palette of colors frequently used by Maxfield Parrish, an advertising design artist for magazines in early 1900's. Being fond of the CMYK colors, he created fine art paintings specifically for the color print market with this color palette. Some consider this to be a primary palette.

This is a good example where color matching does not work. The intense fuchsia color of the flowers in a reference photo is extremely difficult to match. You may find the right shade eventually but only after buying many tubes of RED-VIOLET variations. Find a hue you like and use it! A viewer looking at your painting is not going to know that you did not match the color of the flowers to your reference photo, nor will they care. They will just see the beautiful magenta color you chose.

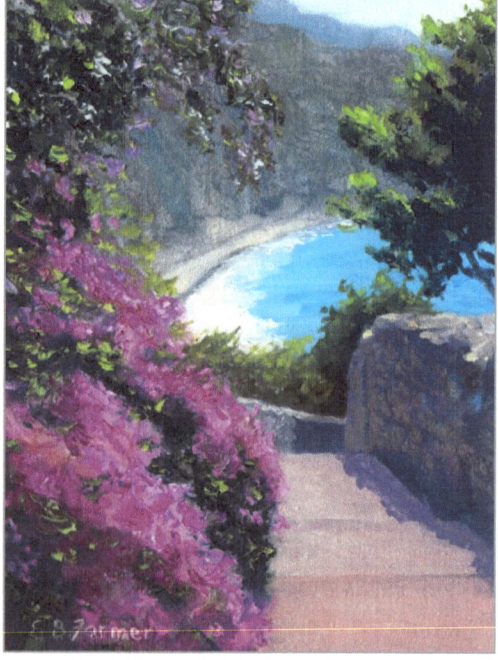

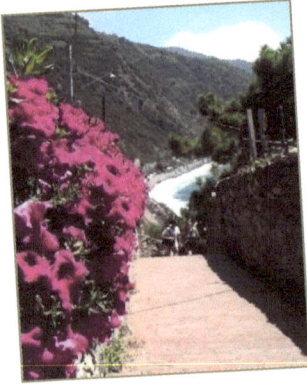

In *A Peek Beyond,* I used Magenta PR122, Cadmium Yellow Medium PY35 and Cyan Blue PB15:3.

A Peek Beyond, *7"x5" oil, private collection*

High Intensity colors in a TRIAD

High intensity or bright color schemes can produce a very up-lifting mood as in the painting *Kendall Pond* below. For this High Intensity Triad, I used Napthol PR112, Lemon Yellow PY3 and Cerulean Blue PB35.

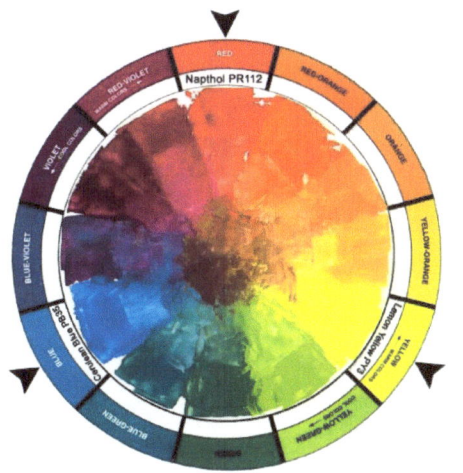

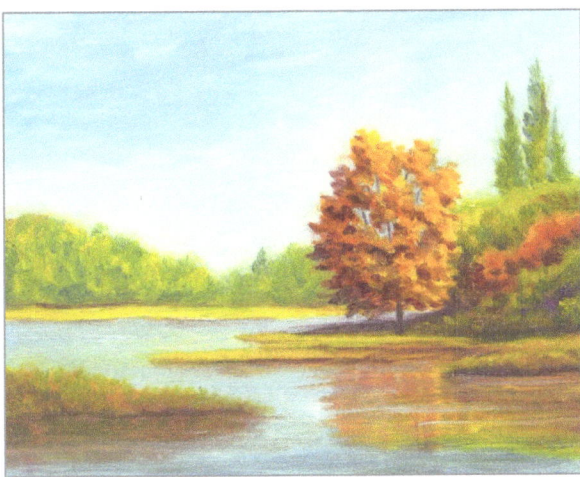

Kendall Pond, *8"x10" oil*
High Intensity Triad color scheme

Low Intensity colors in a TRIAD

Explore a Triadic color scheme using low intensity brown, earth, or neutral colors.

Using a low intensity color scheme, you may find that you prefer a moody feeling to your art. For this version below, of *Kendall Pond,* I used a Low Intensity, Triad color scheme. Colors used were Terra Rosa PR102, Naples Yellow PBr24 and Indanthrone Blue PB60.

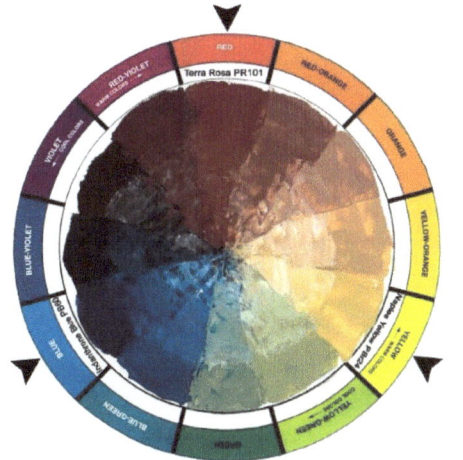

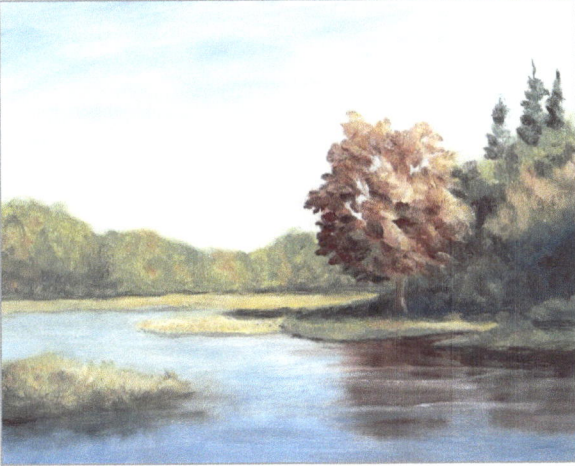

Kendall Pond, *8"x10" oil*
Low Intensity Triad color scheme

Chapter 6
Tetrad Color Schemes

The Tetrad Color Scheme consists of a double pair of Complementary Colors. Complementary colors are any two colors opposite each other on the Color Wheel and they may include primary, secondary, or tertiary pairs. There are nine Tetrad variations possible. Three variations use the square shape, which represents equal spacing between all the colors on the Color Wheel. The other six variations use the rectangle shape on the Color Wheel which represents closer to a Complementary color group of colors.

The Tetrad color scheme is the most varied of color schemes because of its use of two Complementary color pairs and is easy to harmonize. When using this scheme, be sure one color is the dominant color. The Tetrad is useful when multiple vibrant colors are present.

In the following illustrations I have identified the dominant color based on different schemes.

Square Tetrad

The dominant color in *Uphill Path* is RED. Colors used were Cadmium Red Medium PR108, Cadmium Yellow Medium PY35, Permanent Green (mix) and Ultramarine Blue PB29.

The reds in this painting vary from RED-ORANGE at the background to a deeper RED-VIOLET in the foreground. Viridian is altered by using any one or more of the other colors in this scheme.

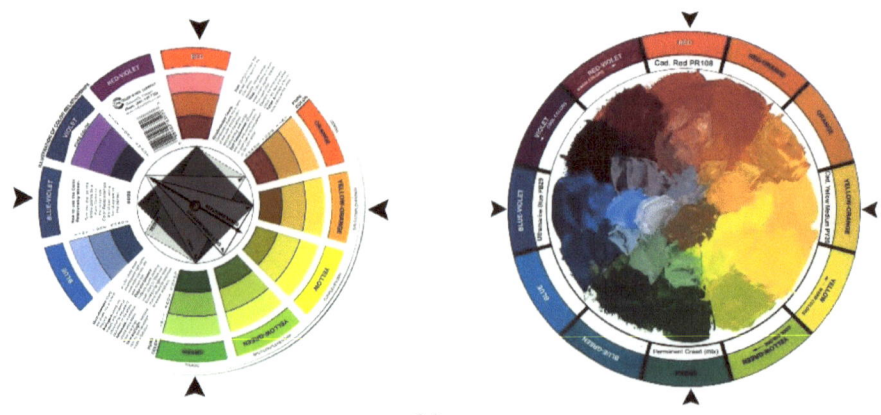

Browns are essentially neutralized ORANGE so to mix a brown, start with YELLOW-ORANGE, add a small amount of RED, then depending on the bias of the brown you want to create, add small amounts of BLUE-VIOLET at a time to create a warm brown (red bias) or GREEN to create a cool brown (blue bias). The degree of neutralized ORANGE or BROWN will depend on the application needed.

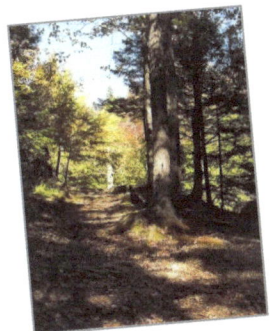
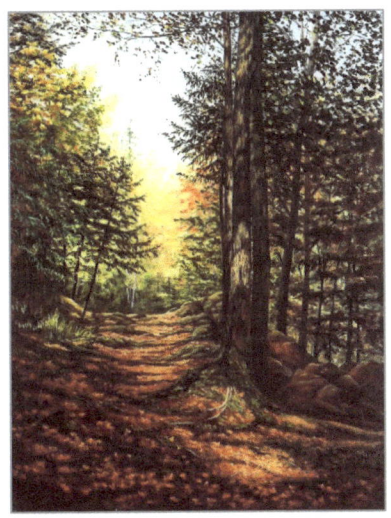

Uphill Path, *24"x18" oil*, private collection

2. The dominant color in *Beach Dune L* is ORANGE with BLUE as the Complementary. Colors used were Magenta PR122, Cadmium Orange PO20, Permanent Yellow Green (mix) and Cobalt Blue PB28.

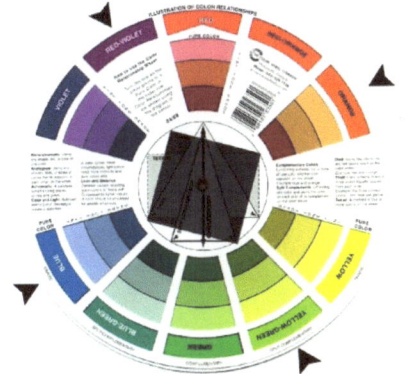

Since this color palette uses no Yellow, the YELLOW-GREEN I used had a strong yellow bias so I could create the warm YELLOW-ORANGE sand color.

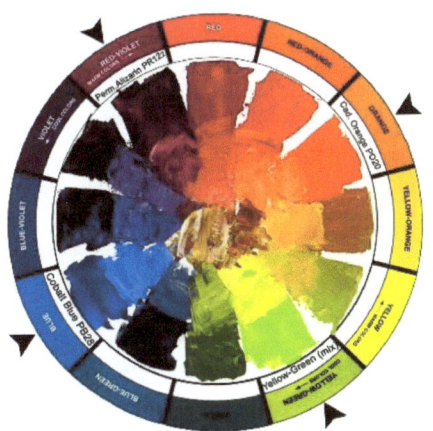
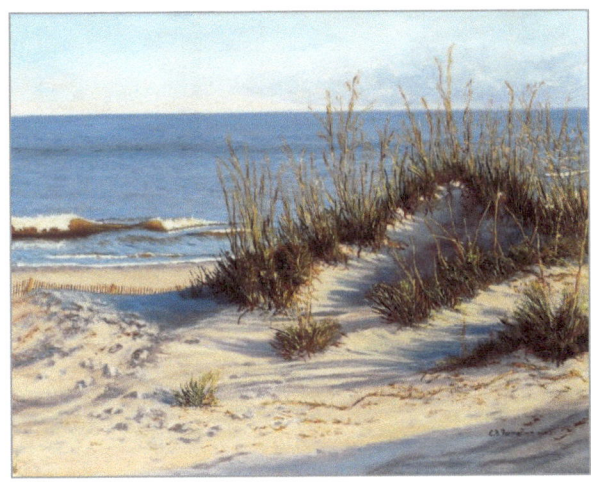

Beach Dune, *16"x20 oil*, private collection

3. The dominant color in *Spike Flowers* is BLUE-GREEN. Colors used were Cadmium Red Light PR108, Hansa Yellow PY3, Phthalo Blue PB15 and Dioxazine Violet PV37.

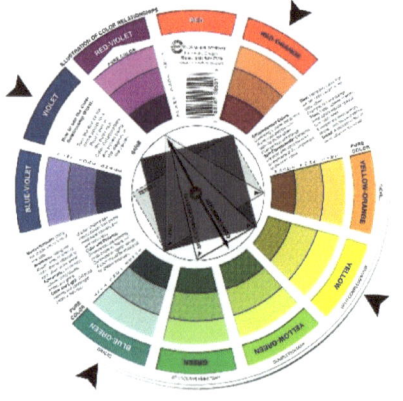

Although this scheme does not offer the use of RED-VIOLET which is shown in the reference photo, the RED-ORANGE and YELLOW colors I used in the painting are still very vibrant against the cool BLUE-GREEN colors. If I had felt that the RED-VIOLET was an important factor in this painting, I would have needed to change color scheme to include the RED-VIOLET.

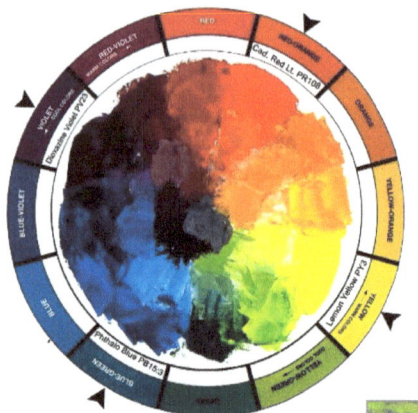

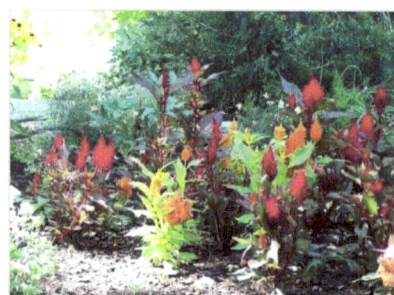

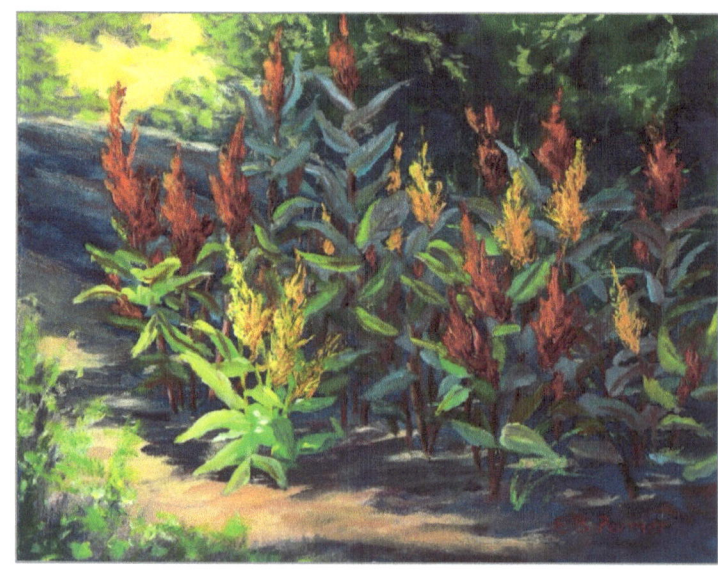

Spike Flowers, *8"x10" oil*

Rectangle Tetrad

1. The dominant color in *Fast Lane* is VIOLET. Colors used were Cadmium Red Deep PR108, Hansa Yellow PY3, Viridian Green PG18 and Dioxazine Violet PV37.

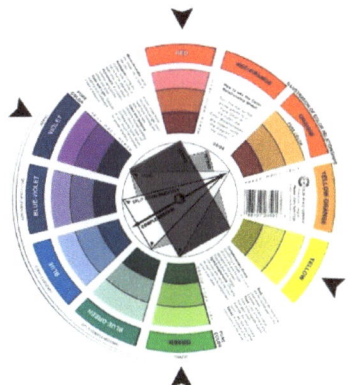
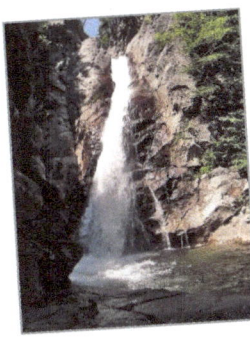
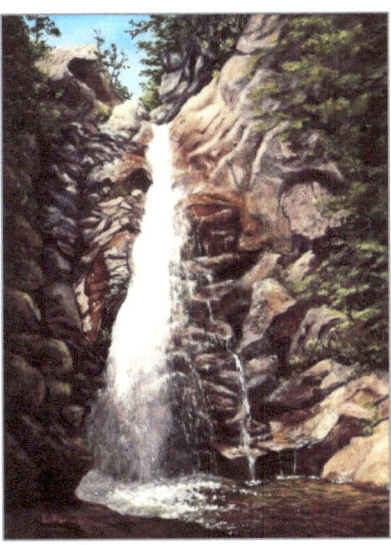

To make the burnt sienna color, I used RED and YELLOW to make an ORANGE first, then I added varying amounts of VIOLET or GREEN to neutralize the colors to varying shades for the rocks' colors.

Fast Lane, *12"x9" oil*

2. The dominant color in *Morning Sunrays* is YELLOW-GREEN. Colors used for this

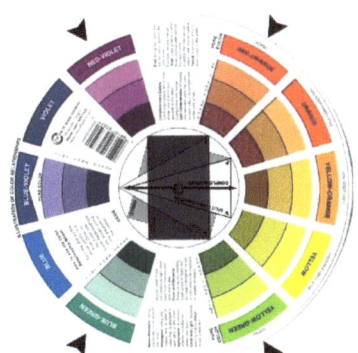

painting were Cadmium Red Light PR108, Permanent Yellow Green (mix), Phthalo Blue PB15 and Permanent Alizarin Crimson PR122.

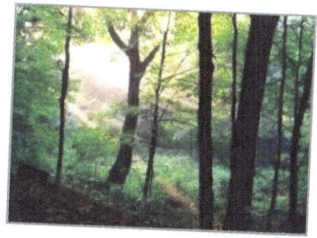

The photograph shows most of the picture being green, but too much green can be monotonous. By opening the scene up just a little and playing up the reddish-brown foreground color which represents old leaves and debris, the other colors can now take on more of a supporting role for the greens.

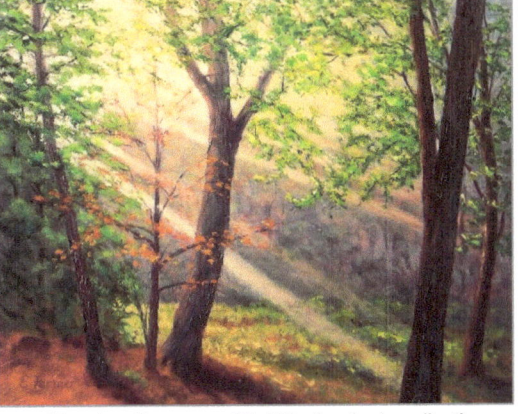

Morning Sunrays, *8"x10" oil, private* collection

3. The dominant color in *Cypress Row* is ORANGE. I used Cadmium Red Medium PR108, Cadmium Orange PO20, Viridian Green PG18 and Cobalt Blue PB28 in this painting.

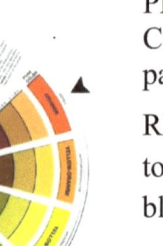

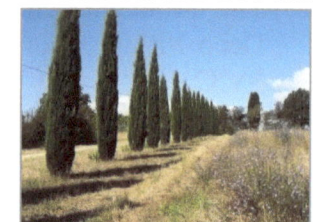

RED and ORANGE are mixed together and neutralized with blue or green for the grass.

The darkest value on the Cypress trees is not black. I created a dark by mixing the GREEN with a small amount of RED, neutralizing the GREEN to a strong dark.

Note: Do not reach for your tube of black when you think you need black but rather, think about what two complementary colors you can use to create a dark color.

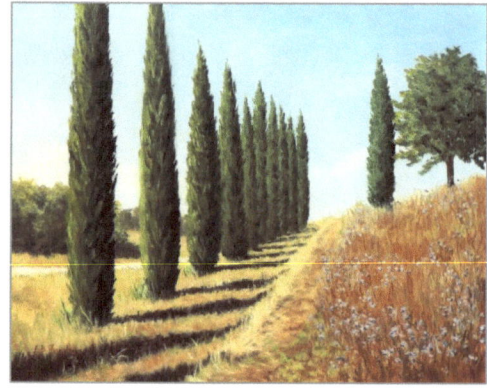

Cypress Row, *11"x14" oil,* private collection

4. The dominant color in *Acadia Coast* is BLUE-GREEN. Colors used in this painting were Cadmium Red Medium PR108, Cadmium Yellow Medium PY35, Phthalo Blue PB15 and Ultramarine Blue PB29.

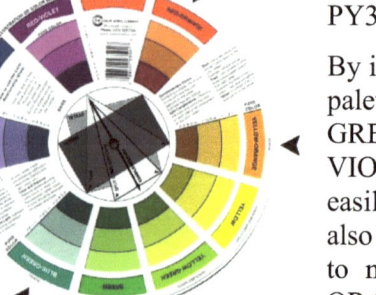

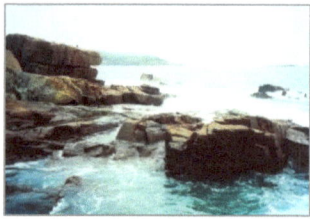

By including two Blues in this palette, it allows the BLUE-GREEN and the BLUE-VIOLET areas to be adjusted easily, using pure pigment. I also used the BLUE-VIOLET to neutralize the YELLOW-ORANGE found throughout the rocks.

This painting could have also been painted using the Complementary palette of ORANGE and BLUE expanding the palette to include the warm and cool of each color i.e., ORANGE would also include YELLOW-ORANGE (warm), RED-ORANGE (cool) and BLUE would include BLUE-GREEN (cool) and BLUE-VIOLET (warm).

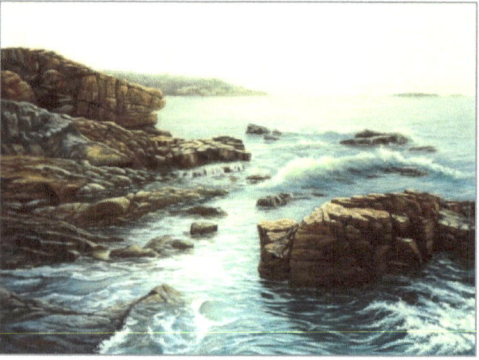

Acadia Coast, *18"x24" oil,* private collection

5. The dominant color in *Water lily* is BLUE. Colors used were Quinacridone Violet PV19, Cadmium Orange PO20, Cobalt Blue PB28 and Cadmium Yellow Light PY35.

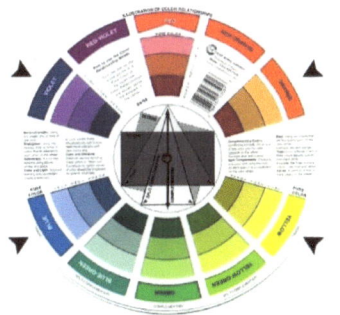

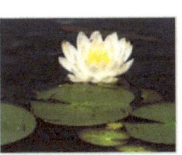 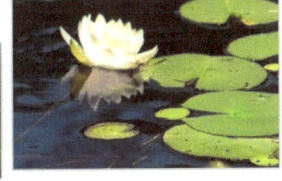

To darken the blue colors and create variations, I used VIOLET. The VIOLET also shows up in the water reflection of the lily as a soft lilac color. The VIOLET I used in this painting had a stronger reddish bias.

The dull green is mixed by starting with a green mixture of BLUE and YELLOW and adding ORANGE or VIOLET to alter the warm or cool of the green.

Note: For *Waterlily*, two different photographs were used. One photograph shows off the beautiful sky reflection and the pattern of lily pads. The close-up photo of the lily is used for the portrait of the lily. This is another instance where one photograph may not be sufficient to compose a beautiful painting.

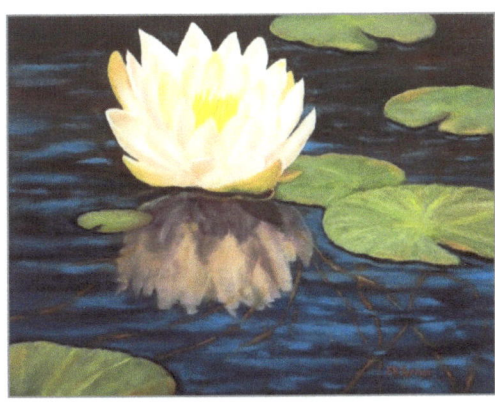

Waterlily, *11"x14" oil,* private collection

6. The dominant color in *Amor Caritas* is YELLOW-ORANGE.

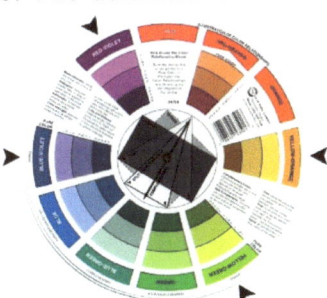

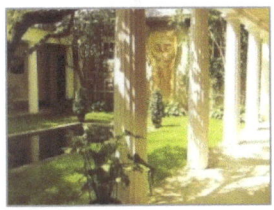

Colors used were Magenta PR122 (Quinacridone), Cadmium Yellow PY35, Permanent Yellow Green (mix) and Ultramarine Blue PB29. Although some areas have RED-VIOLET undertones, I chose the YELLOW-ORANGE as the dominant color. YELLOW-GREEN is a significant color throughout the area, further strengthening the choice for this color scheme.

If you are using reference that makes it difficult to find the dominant color, you may have to select one that makes the most sense and be mindful of that choice throughout your painting.

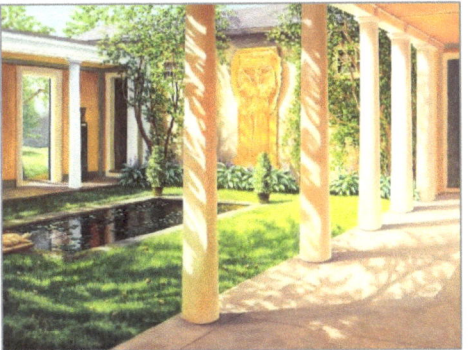

Amor Caritas, *18"x24" oil*

Chapter 7
Complementary Color Schemes

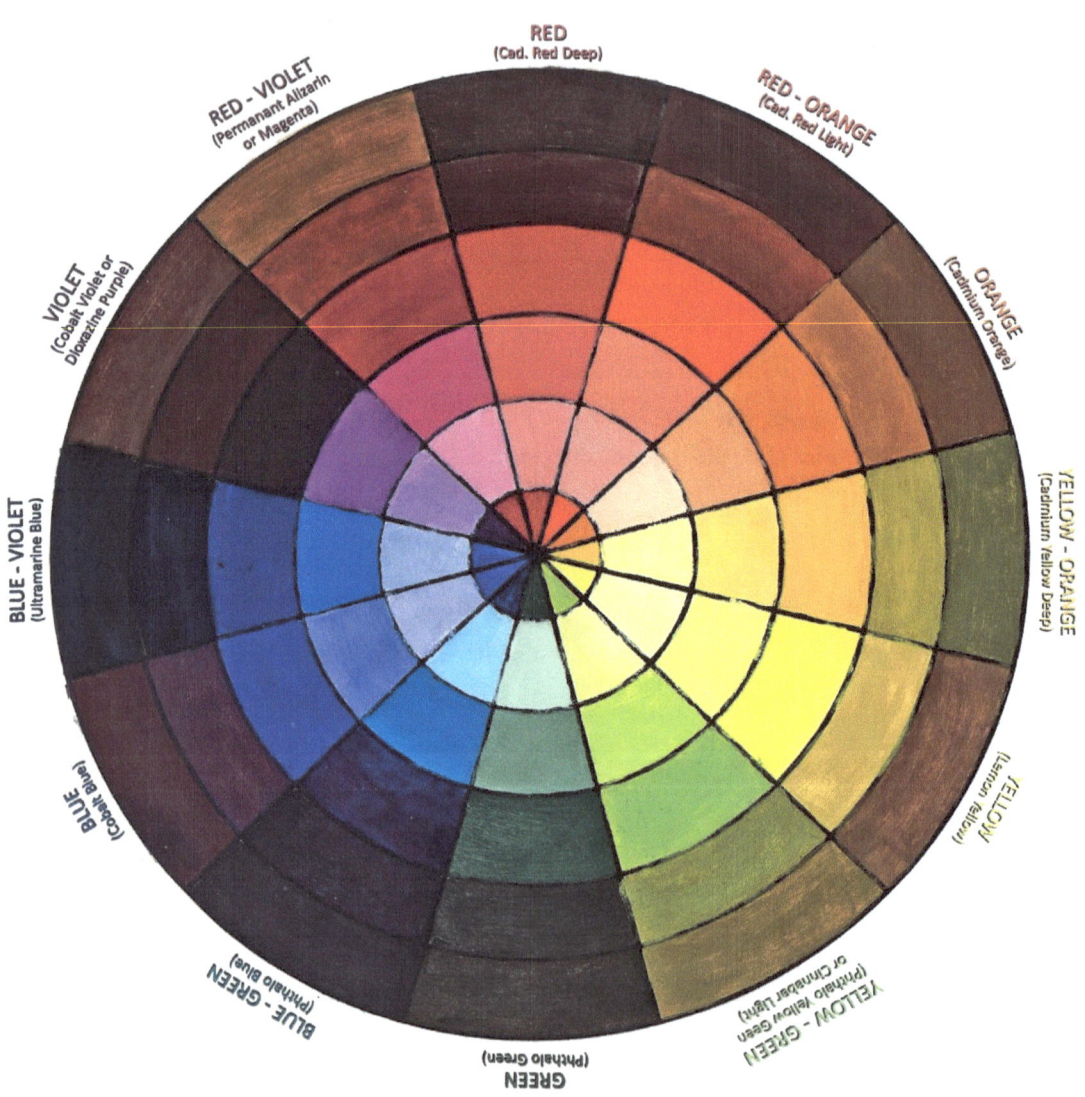

RED
(Cad. Red Deep)

RED - VIOLET
(Permanant Alizarin
or Magenta)

RED - ORANGE
(Cad. Red Light)

VIOLET
(Cobalt Violet or
Dioxazine Purple)

ORANGE
(Cadmium Orange)

BLUE - VIOLET
(Ultramarine Blue)

YELLOW - ORANGE
(Cadmium Yellow Deep)

BLUE
(Cobalt Blue)

YELLOW
(Lemon Yellow)

BLUE - GREEN
(Phthalo blue)

YELLOW - GREEN
(Phthalo Yellow Green
or Cinnabar Light)

GREEN
(Phthalo Green)

Complementary Color Schemes

Complimentary spelled with an "i" means flattering, where in art, complementary spelled with an "e" refers to any two colors opposite each other on the Color Wheel. When you mix two colors directly opposite each other on the Color Wheel, the result will be the neutralization of these colors. RED/GREEN, YELLOW/VIOLET and ORANGE/BLUE are examples of Complementary pairs, but tertiary colors may also be used to create a Complementary palette.

When mixing colors opposite each other on the Color Wheel, these color combinations cancel the original color pigments in each contributing color, which creates beautiful neutrals or chromatic darks. I prefer to not use the term gray as it implies the use of black and white. You may not always be able to identify the contributing colors, but you should be able to find a dominant color. By mixing your own neutrals, you will keep the harmony in your painting.

When using a Complementary color scheme, you may expand your color choices to include the warm and cool of each Complementary color for a total of six colors. I used the extended Complementary color palette for all the examples below.

Only one Complementary color group can be the dominant color in a painting.

"Primary colors look brightest when they are brought into contrast with their Complementary." —Claude Monet

Practice: Mix colors on a Color Wheel, with its complement, to discover the range of neutrals you might create. Add white to reveal the lighter values of these colors.

The Complementary color scheme of the Kendall Pond painting below is Orange/Blue. The complementary colors used include the warm and cool of each complementary color which are found on either side of the complement color. Orange colors - Cad. Orange PO20, Cad. Yellow Med. PY35 (warm) and Cad. Red Light PR108 (cool). Blue colors - Cobalt Blue Deep PB28, Phthalo Blue PB15:3 (cool) and Ultramarine Blue PB29 warm).

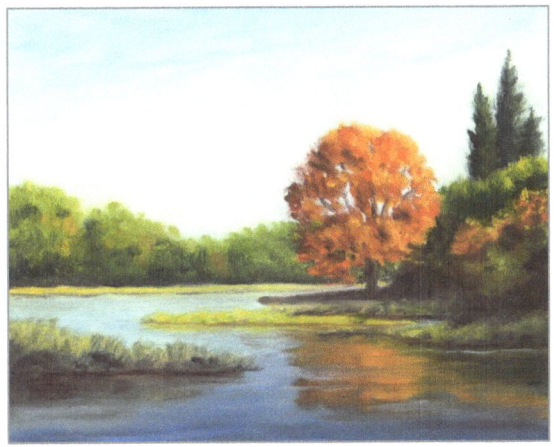

Kendall Pond, *8"x10" oil*
Complementary color scheme

RED/GREEN Complementary Color Scheme

Living in New England, nature continually calls me especially in summertime with all the lush green as in *Garden at Prescott Park* below.

Colors used for this painting were Permanent Alizarin Crimson PR122 Cadmium Red Deep PR108, Cadmium Red Lt. PR108, Phthalo Blue PB15:3Permanent, Permanent. Green PG36 and Yellow Green (mix).

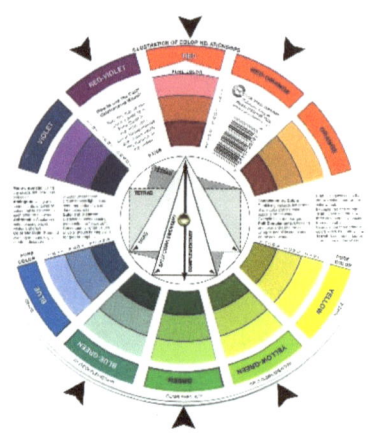

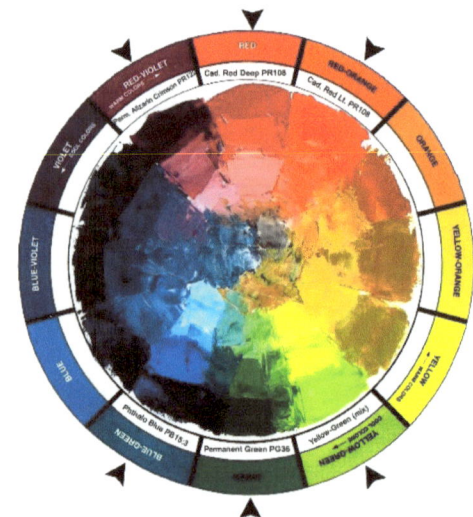

With GREEN as the obvious dominant color, this group of Complementary colors works well with each other to create an array of beautiful garden colors.

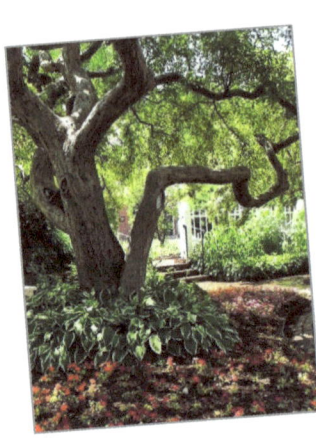

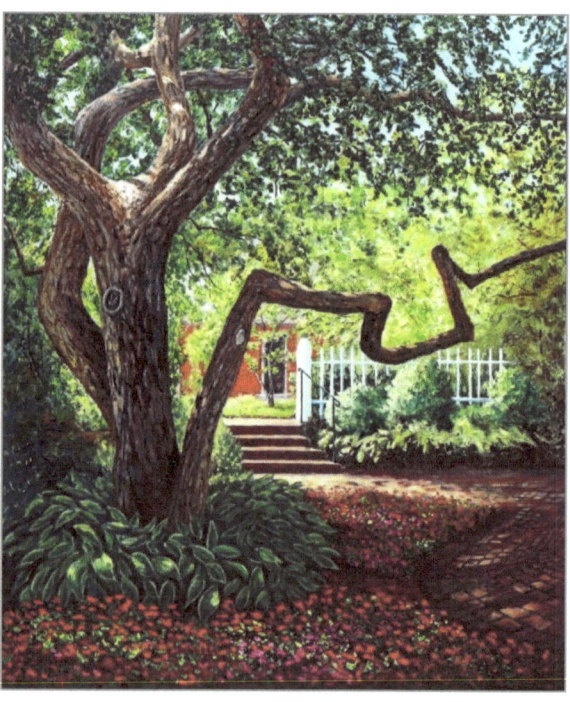

Garden at Prescott Park, *24"x20" oil*

ORANGE/BLUE Complementary Color Scheme

ORANGE is the dominant color in this example but presents itself as a dominant neutralized ORANGE, similar to Burnt Sienna.

Colors used for this painting were Cadmium Red Lt PR108, Cadmium Orange PO20, Cadmium Yellow Med PY35, Ultramarine Blue PB29, Cobalt Blue PB28 and Phthalo Blue PB15:3.

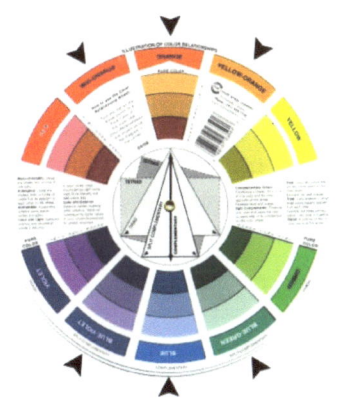

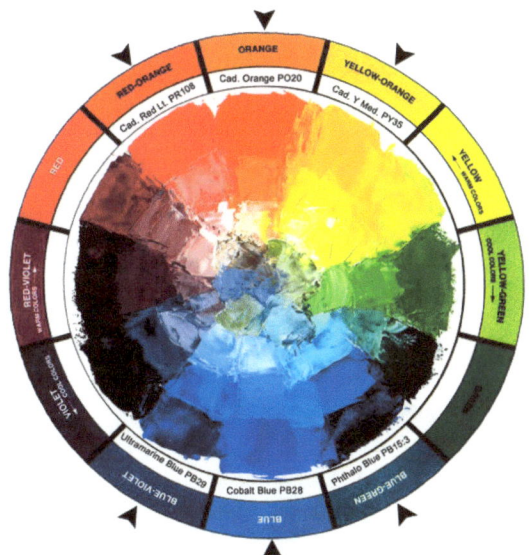

The blue colors were neutralized using the orange complements. In *Bermuda Sunset below*, I could have also considered using a tertiary Complementary scheme with RED-ORANGE being the dominant color and BLUE-GREEN being the complement, but this would have excluded the use of the YELLOW-ORANGE which, may have changed the outcome of the scheme of the painting.

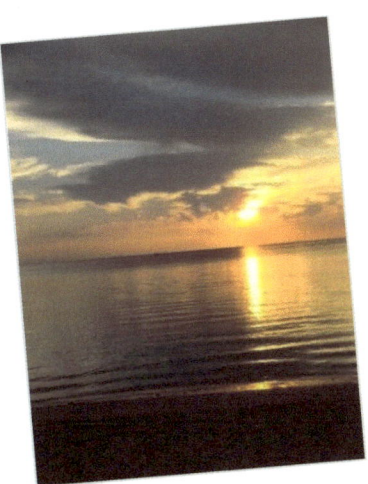

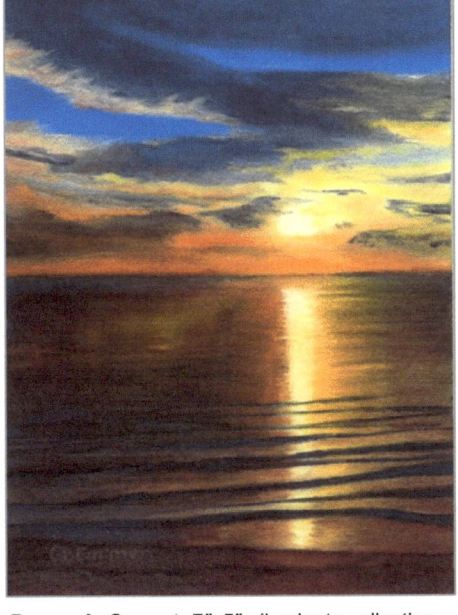

Bermuda Sunset, *7"x5" oil,* private collection

YELLOW/VIOLET Complementary Color Scheme

In *Morning Commute below*, VIOLET is the dominant color in this scheme with YELLOW being its complement.

Colors used in this painting were Cadmium Yellow Med. PY35, Lemon Yellow PY3, Yellow Green (mix), Perm Alizarin Crimson PR122, Dioxazine Violet PV23 and Ultramarine Blue PB29.

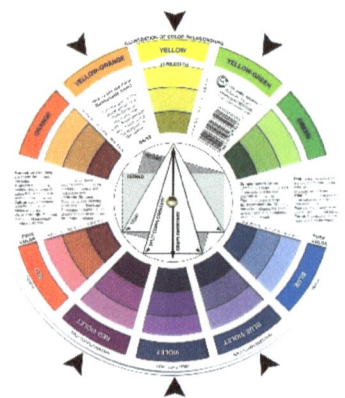

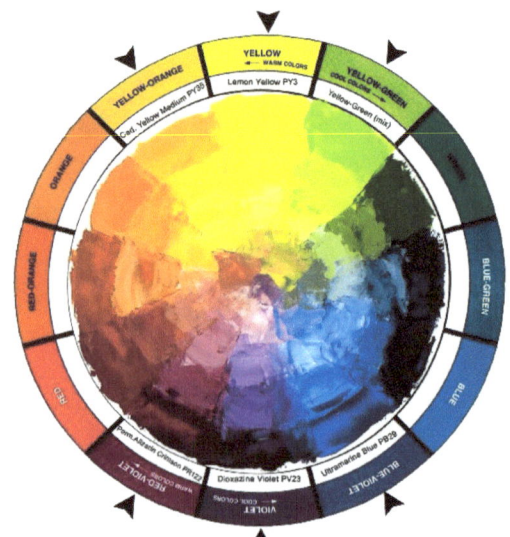

Using an extended Complementary palette, gave me all the colors needed to render this painting. Note the wide range of VIOLET variations used throughout the painting. Most of the Yellows used read as the cool YELLOW-GREEN.

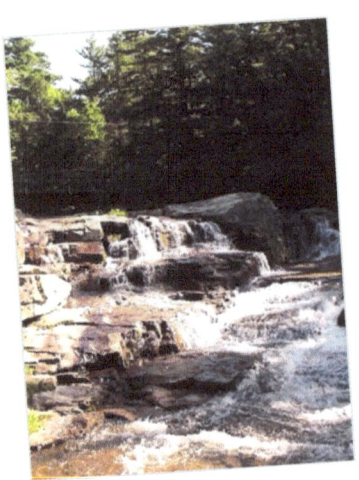

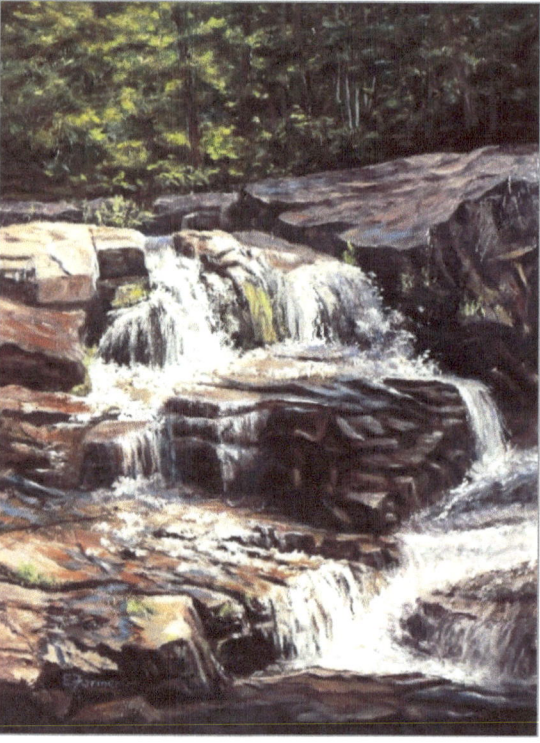

Morning Commute, *12"x9" oil,* private collection

Chapter 8
Split Complementary and Analogous Complementary Color Schemes

Split Complementary

A Split Complementary color scheme uses any color with the split-complementary using two colors on each side of its complement. Example: If RED is the complement of GREEN, a Split Complementary color scheme uses a color on each side of its complement i.e. YELLOW-GREEN and BLUE-GREEN are positioned on either side of GREEN. This provides high contrast with less tension of the complementary color scheme.

The illustrations in the following pages for Split Complementary color schemes have a dominant color named for each reference photo which will help you to visualize color mixing possibilities. For each of the photo references, however, you might choose a different Split Complementary combination. There is no absolute right or wrong in the combination choices, it just comes down to what your color scheme preference is.

Analogous Complementary Color Schemes

An Analogous color scheme uses colors that are adjacent to each other on the Color Wheel. You can use at least two but no more than five consecutive colors on the wheel to be considered an Analogous color scheme. Example: if RED is the dominant color, the Analogous complementary colors would be YELLOW, YELLOW-GREEN, GREEN, BLUE-GREEN and BLUE.

I have included the color names that would make the Split Complementary scheme an Analogous Complementary color scheme. These additional colors are dependent solely on your need on an individual basis for a painting. An example is that you may not need all the colors in a five color Analogous Complementary scheme if a pair of the colors could be used to make one of the five colors needed i.e. YELLOW and BLUE makes GREEN so you may decide not to use green at all.

RED as the dominant color

YELLOW-GREEN is the only yellow in this *Hollyhock* photo. YELLOW-GREEN will need to have a strong yellow bias in order to use it to warm the highlights in the reds. BLUE-GREEN mixed with RED will give you the variations for the shadows.

For the green colors in the photo below, mix the YELLOW-GREEN and the BLUE-GREEN adding RED to create the variations of greens needed.

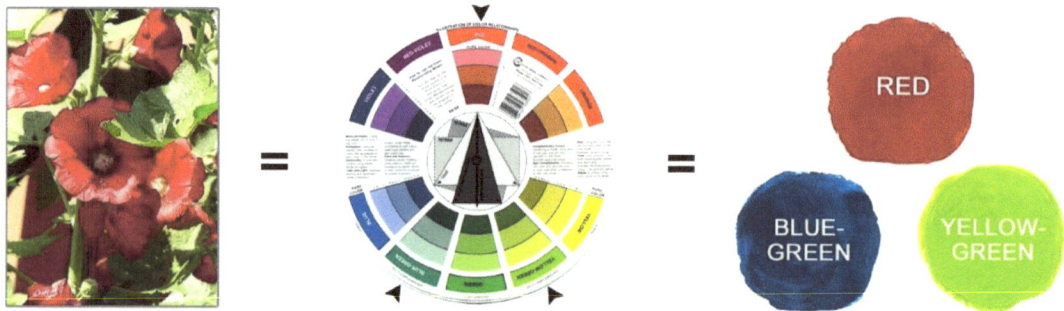

Add any combination of BLUE, GREEN and/or YELLOW to make this an Analogous Complementary color scheme.

RED-ORANGE as the dominant color

RED-ORANGE will represent all the warm hues in a painting of *Red Leaves*. Since this split complementary color scheme is void of any yellow, you would need to choose a RED-ORANGE with a strong yellow bias. You may not exactly get a gold color from this scheme, but you would be able to paint this with some similarity to the photo adjusting through tints and values.

Select a GREEN with a yellow bias like a Phthalo Green PG7 to allow for warmer and lighter greens. Choosing your color bias for will depends on your desired outcome but by simply adjusting the bias of the contributing colors, you can achieve a fair resemblance of the colors you need.

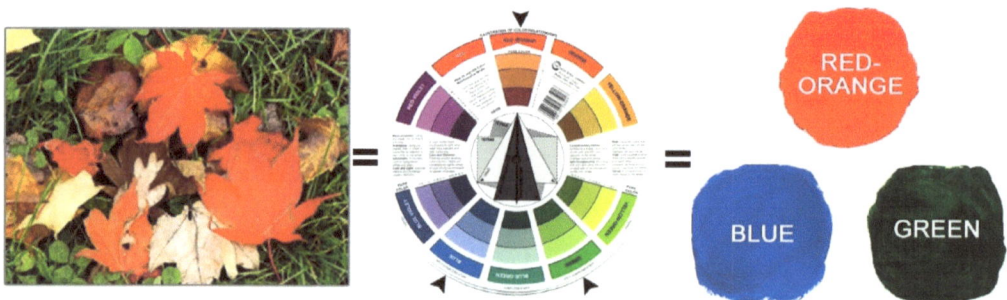

Add any combination of BLUE-VIOLET, BLUE-GREEN and/or YELLOW-GREEN to make this an Analogous Complementary color scheme.

ORANGE as the dominant color

ORANGE is the dominant color for *Orange Tree*. You may think that with no yellow on your palette, you will not be able to make green but if you choose an ORANGE with a strong yellow bias and a BLUE-GREEN PG15:3 (GS) with a yellow bias, there will be enough yellow from the two contributing colors to make a nice green for the trees.

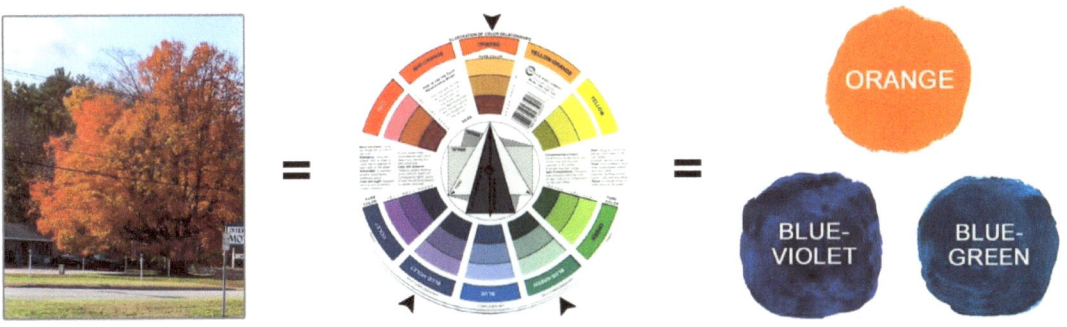

Add any combination of VIOLET, BLUE, and/or YELLOW-GREEN to make this an Analogous Complementary color scheme.

YELLOW-ORANGE as the dominant color

This color scheme for the *Mountain River* is close to a primary color scheme. Mixing your colors in this reference photo would be straightforward with this Split-Complementary scheme. Choose a YELLOW-ORANGE with a strong yellow bias and/or choose a RED-ORANGE to have a strong red bias depending on your desire for the outcome for the painting.

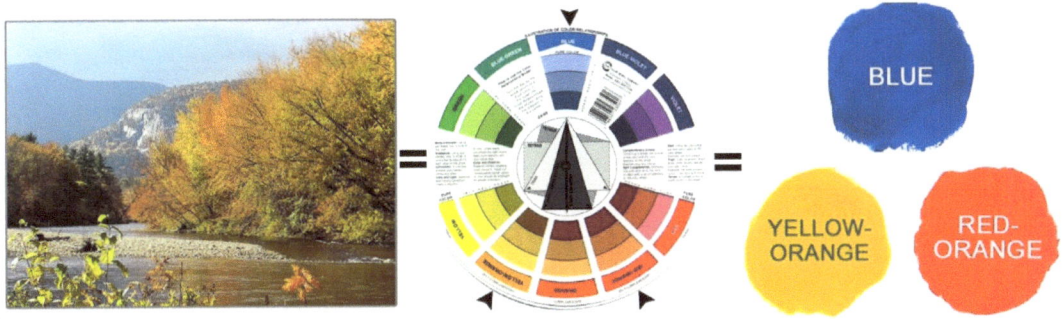

Add any combination of YELLOW, RED-ORANGE and/or RED to make this an Analogous Complementary color scheme.

YELLOW as the dominant color

Subtle, olive colored greens seen in the *Bridge and Yellow Tree* photo can be mixed using the YELLOW and BLUE-VIOLET. You would not be able to mix a bright green with this color scheme due to the red bias in the BLUE-VIOLET but for this example, you would not need a bright green. The RED-VIOLET would be used to mix a warmer Yellow color.

For sky color, BLUE-VIOLET plus a small amount of YELLOW could offer you a suitable sky color although it may not be as bright as you may like.

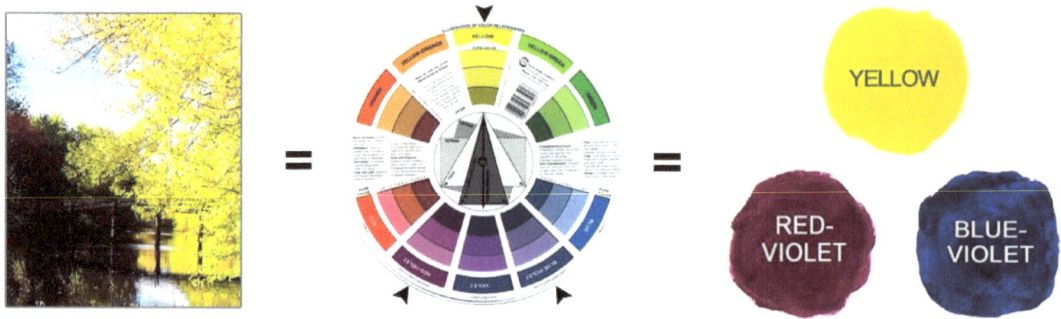

Add any combination of RED, VIOLET and/or BLUE to make this an Analogous Complementary color scheme.

YELLOW-GREEN as the dominant color

This *Marsh* photo offers an array of beautiful neutrals. Choose a YELLOW-GREEN with a strong yellow bias since this is the only yellow you would have to mix with. To mix any kind of orange color as in the marsh area, use YELLOW-GREEN and RED. For the distant trees, mix YELLOW-GREEN and VIOLET.

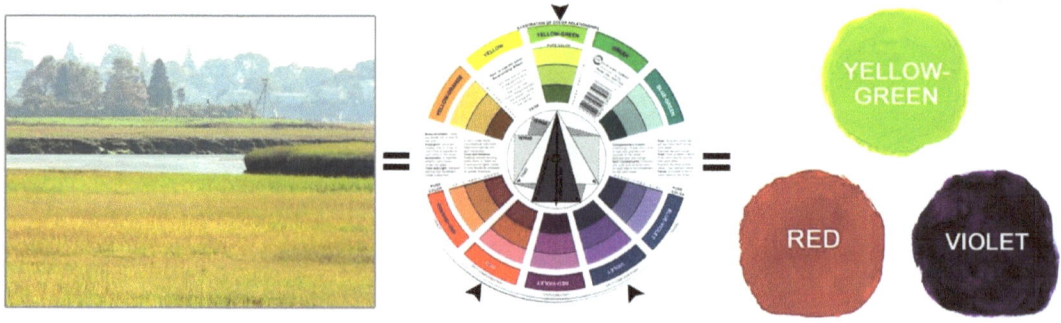

Add any combination of RED-ORANGE, RED-VIOLET and/or BLUE-VIOLET to make this an Analogous Complementary color scheme.

GREEN as the dominant color

The photo reference for this *Country Barn* shows mostly green. The RED-ORANGE will need to have a strong yellow bias to enable you to create green variations. The red barn can be mixed with a combination of any of these colors. Browns (fence) and Neutrals (rocks) can be mixed using green with either of the red colors.

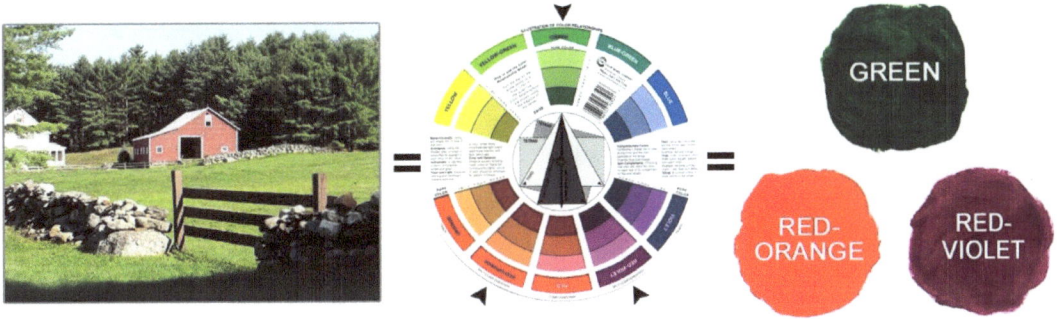

Add any combination of ORANGE, RED and/or BLUE-VIOLET to make this an Analogous Complementary color scheme.

BLUE-GREEN as the dominant color

This *Cape Elizabeth Lighthouse* photo readily shows all the colors to be used in this color scheme. The bias of this BLUE-GREEN may not be important since the water is not tropical. Since there is no yellow in this scheme though, you would choose an ORANGE with a good strong yellow bias, to mix greens.

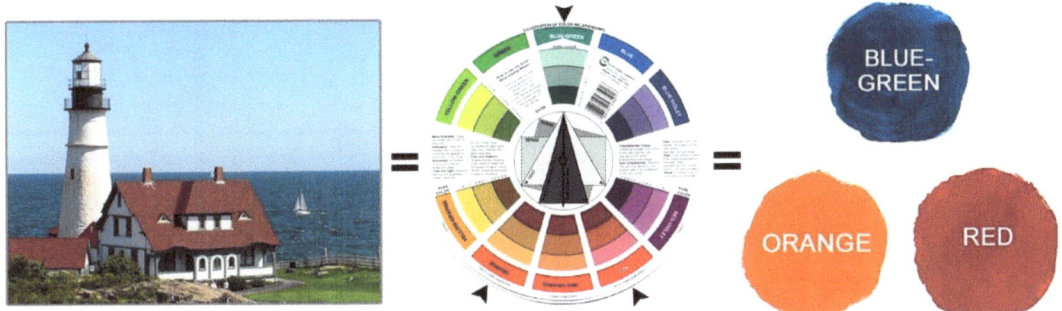

Add any combination of YELLOW-ORANGE, RED-ORANGE and/or RED-VIOLET, to make this an Analogous Complementary color scheme.

BLUE as the dominant color

The *Italian Coast* photo below reads as an almost Monochromatic blue color scheme but it does have variations of BLUE with the accent of the pink colored houses on the cliff. Mixing neutrals for the cliffs is achievable by using all three colors.

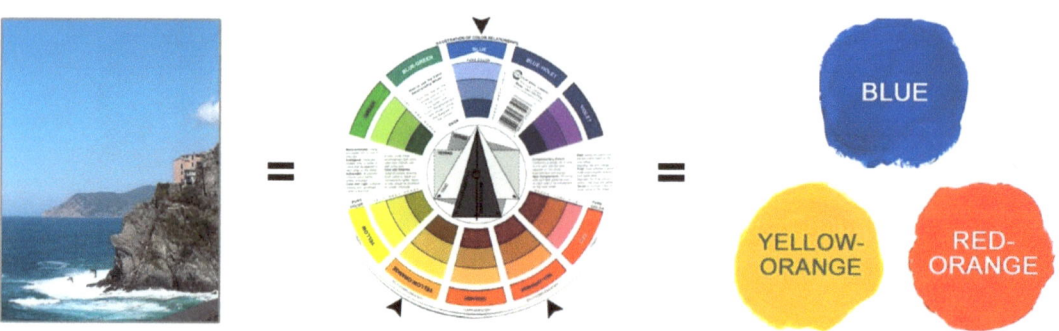

Add any combination of YELLOW, ORANGE and/or RED to make this an Analogous Complementary color scheme.

BLUE-VIOLET as the dominant color

The *Mt. Chocorua* photo reference suggests a near Complementary group of colors (blue/orange). The darks in the reference photo look black but mixes of blue plus ORANGE and/or YELLOW will create colorful neutral darks giving the cool feel of this late Fall New England day.

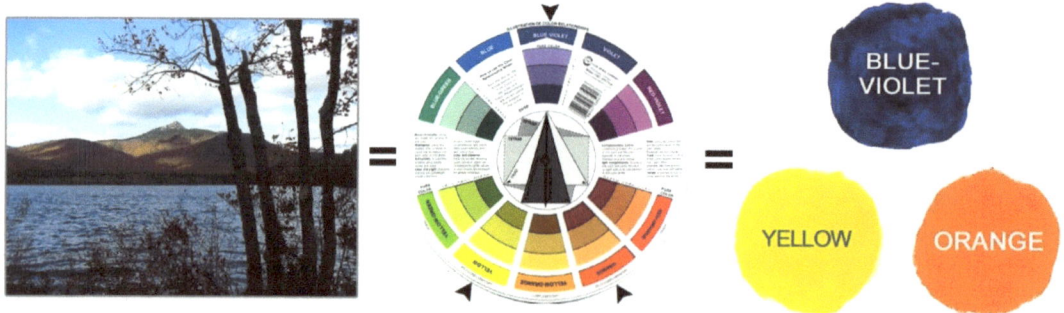

Add any combination of YELLOW-GREEN, YELLOW-ORANGE and/or RED-ORANGE to make this an Analogous Complementary color scheme.

VIOLET as the dominant color

The VIOLET used in this *Mountain Lupine* photo might need to have a red bias since the Lupine is a Red-Violet. Mixing greens with either of the two yellows will produce some interesting dull green variations for the distant trees. Use more YELLOW-GREEN in the foreground foliage so it will be brighter and stand out against the dull olive-green colors in the distant trees.

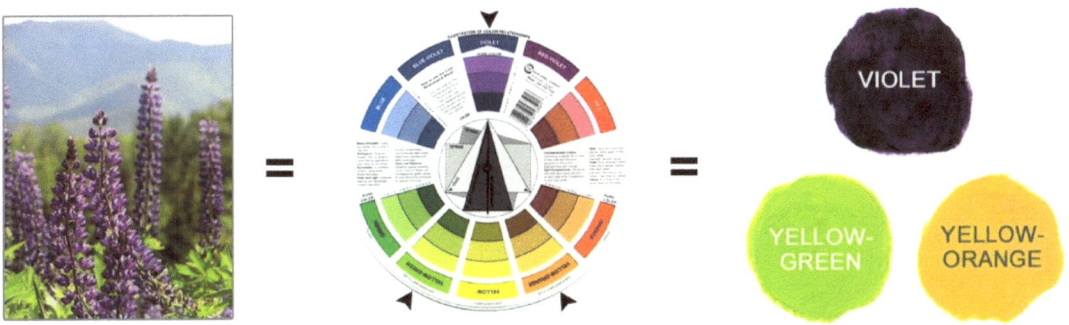

Add any combination of GREEN, YELLOW, and/or ORANGE to make this an Analogous Complementary color scheme.

RED-VIOLET as the dominant color

The RED-VIOLET in *Bird on Branch* can be neutralized using a combination of the other two contributing colors plus white. With the use of the primary color YELLOW, you would be able to achieve all your colors needed for a painting.

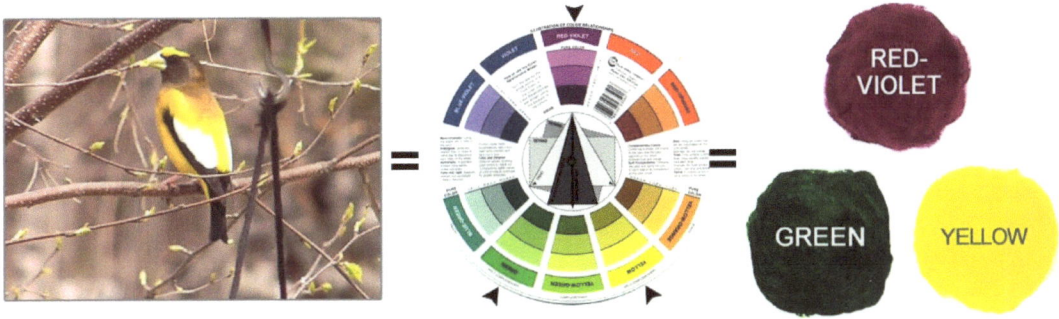

Add any combination of BLUE-GREEN, YELLOW-GREEN and/or YELLOW-ORANGE to make this an Analogous Complementary color scheme.

Chapter 9
Analogous and Monochromatic
Color Schemes

VIOLET Analogous Color Scheme (3 colors)

In this *Serene Dingy* photo, the dominant color is VIOLET with the other two contributing colors offering a warm and cool version. White is used to lighten all the pure colors. You could also start with high intensity versions of these colors where you may not even need to use white. Using the three-color analogous scheme can bring a serene feeling to the painting as seen in the reference photo. The overall light value in this reference photo also helps to give this scene a calming effect.

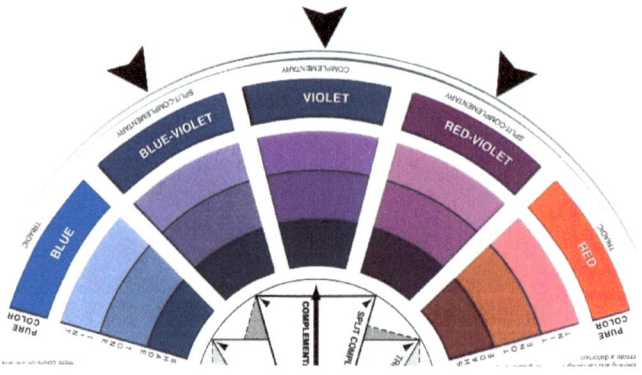

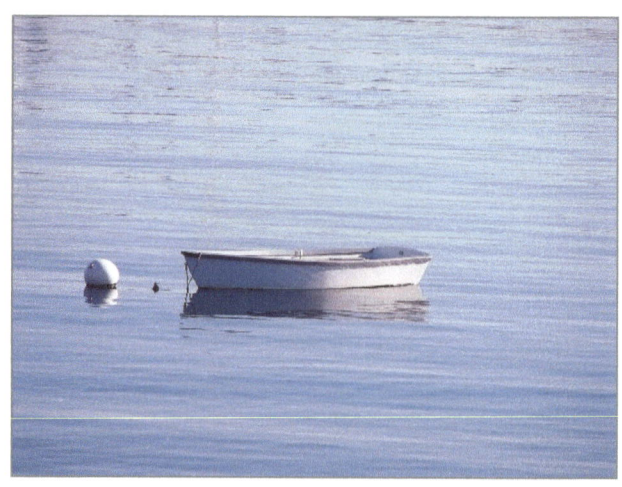

RED Analogous Color Schemes (5 colors)

The dominant color in this *Vibrant Sunset* photo is RED-ORANGE although some of the variations are a light tint or neutralized. The suggested analogous colors scheme might include up to five colors.

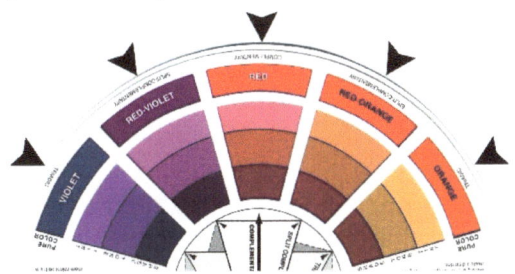

To make a dark neutral color for the silhouetted areas mix VIOLET and ORANGE. You do not have to use all five of these colors and you can always adjust any of the colors bias to suit your need i.e., Orange might need to have a strong YELLOW-ORANGE bias.

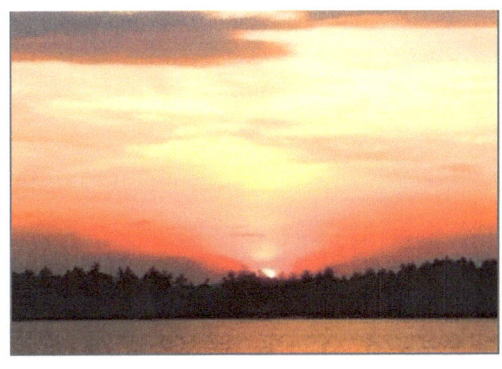

Monochromatic Color Scheme

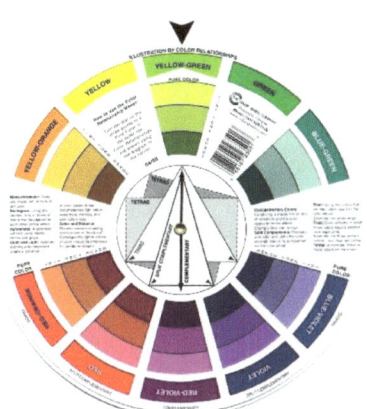

The monochromatic color in the photo *Green Meadow Morning* has variations of lights and darks using a single color, altering the saturation through tints (using white) and shade (using black). This scheme looks clean and elegant. Monochromatic colors produce a quieting soothing effect. The monochromatic scheme is very easy on the eyes, especially with blue or green hues.

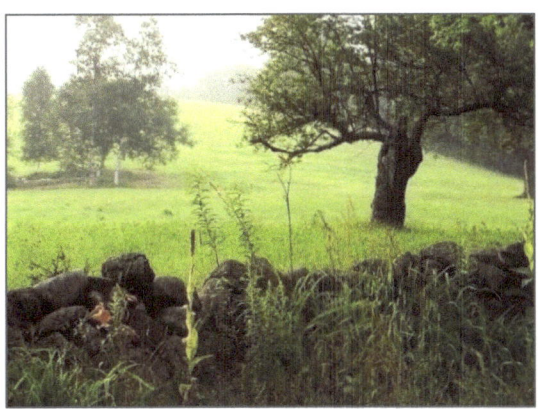

Although each of these examples has traces of other colors, you could practice this monochromatic color scheme and always add an accent color in the end if you choose as in the orange day lilies below.

Afterword

New Habits

• Reach for the Color Wheel each time you are starting a new project and plan your color scheme.

• Choose your color scheme based on a dominant color.

• Choose your color bias based on the mood you want to create for each painting.

• Pre-test your colors on a color card before you start your painting. It is far more frustrating to discover halfway through your painting that the colors you chose are not working for you.

Freedom to Play

• Explore different color schemes.

• Discover what colors can be produced using a simple Triad color scheme. You will get to know these colors more intimately if you explore one group at a time.

• DO stray from your traditional tube colors and treat yourself to new ones occasionally.

• Choose a brighter intensity color scheme using high key colors.

• Choose an all neutral color scheme using low intensity colors.

• Create color cards with new schemes you may have not have thought to use before.

• Use your instincts to trigger what color schemes excite you.

• Select a color scheme for its symbolic reasons to create a theme based painting.

• Add convenience colors as you gain confidence in color mixing.

• Color is for expressing mood, feelings and connecting with the viewer.

• Color schemes offer an infinite combination, and you will learn this through practice.

• Do not be a slave to the brand recommendations in this book. They are intended to be only suggestions.

• Experiment with the colors you currently have; purchase only the colors you need and use only what is necessary.

Building Your Reference Library

• Complete your inventory of colors and keep them handy to identify color biases when starting a new project.

• Continue adding to your color cards and keep them handy for when you may use them again for another project with the same color scheme. Simply review the color card and possibly add to it for your next project.

• Build a library of reference charts that you will use for a lifetime.

The Path of Knowledge

Color theory is a set of principles, not hard and fast rules. When you understand the principles of using the basic twelve colors and their bias, you will gain freedom to choose your own schemes based on a systematic approach, adding your own expressive intuition to the mix.

There are many color schemes to choose from. As you begin experimenting with them, you will discover what you like or do not like and this will help you to produce works of art more simply, creating a connection with your viewer and sharing your story.

My wish for you is that after having read this book you will have gained a new confidence in it which will lead to endless discoveries of your own.

"Go confidently in the direction of your dreams! Live the life you have imagined. As you simplify your life, the laws of the universe will be simpler".

—Henry David Thoreau

Color Index Number	Color Index Name	Swatch	Color Description	Alternative Names	Permanence	Transparent Opaque	Toxicity
RED							
PR102 LK	Natural Iron Oxide		Brownish red with yellow to violet undertones	English Red, Indian Red, Iron Oxide Red, Light Red, Terra Rosa	I*	O-T	A
PR106	Vermillion (genuine)		Bright yellow red	Chinese Vermillion, Cinnabar (natural); French or Genuine Vermillion	I	O	C
PR108	Cadmium Red		Orange red to deep violet red	Cadmium Red Lt, Cadmium Red Med., Cadmium Red Deep, Cadmium Scarlet	I	O	B
PR 108:1	Cadmium-Barium Red		Orange to deep red	Cadmium Red Light, Cadmium Red Medium, Cadmium Red Deep	I	O	B
PR112 HK	Naphthol AS-D		Intense bright scarlet	Azo Red Medium, Bright Red; Naphthol Red; Perm. Red; Scarlet; Vermilion hue	I	SO-ST	A
PR149	Perylene Red BX		Bluish red	Bright Red, Crimson Lake, Perylene Red, Scarlet, Winsor Red Deep	I	ST	A
PR206 LK	Quinacridone Burnt Scarlet		Dark Orange to violet Brown	Permanent Alizarin Crimson, Quinacridone Burnt Orange	I	T	A
PR254 HK	Pyrrole Red		Bright mid-shade red	Bright Red, Pyrrol Red, Pyrrole Red, Scarlet, Sennelier Red, Winsor Red	I	SO	A
RED-ORANGE							
PR101 LK	Synthetic Iron Oxide Red		Brownish shades yellow to orange to red	Brt Sienna, Caput Mortuum, Eng. Red, Indian Red, Burnt Sienna, Raw Umber	I	O-T	A
PR108	Cadmium Red		Orange red to deep violet red; vary by brand	Cadmium Red Light or Medium, Cadmium Scarlet, Selenium Red	I	O	B
PR 108:1	Cadmium-Barium		Orange to deep red	Cadmium Red, Light or Medium	I	O	B
PR168	Anthradquinone Scarlet		Bright yellow red	Anthradquinone Red or Scarlet, Helio, Permanent Red, Scarlet Lake Extra	I - II	SO	B
PR188 HK	Naphthol Scarlet Lake		Bright yellowish red	Chinese Red, Geranium Lake, Naphthol Vermilion, Scarlet Lake	I - II	SO	B
PR251 HK	Pyrazolo-Quinazolone Scarlet		Light bright red	Permanent Red, Vermilion Extra	I	O	A
PR255 HK	Pyrrole Scarlet		Bright red	Coral Red, Perm. Red Med, Pyrrol Scarlet, Pyrrole Vermilion, Scarlet Lake	I	SO	A
ORANGE							
PO5	Hansa Orange RN		Bright reddish orange	Azo Orange, Hansa Orange, Permanent Red Orange	II*	ST	A
PO20	Cadmium Orange		Bright yellowish thru to reddish orange	Cadmium Orange, Cadmium Yellow Deep	I	O	B

Color Index Number	Color Index Name	Swatch	Color Description	Alternative Names	Permanence	Transparent Opaque	Toxicity
ORANGE							
PO34	Pyrazolone Orange		Bright orange to orangish red	Azo Red, Scheveningen Red Scarlet, Vermilion	II*	SO-ST	A
PO43	Perinone Orange		Mid to red shade orange	Brilliant Orange, Perinone Orange, Perm. Orange, Perm. Red Orange	I	SO	A
PO62 LK	Benzimid-azolone Orange H5G		Light yellowish to mid-orange	Azo Orange, Benzimidazolone Orange, Cadmium Orange hue, Perm. Orange	I	SO	A
PO67	Pyrazolo-quinazolone Orange		Saturated red-orange	Brilliant Orange, Coral Orange, Mono Azo Orange	I	O-SO	A
PO73 HK	Pyrrol Orange		Light bright saturated red shade orange	Bright Orange, Irgazin Orange, Perm. Orange, Scarlet Pyrrol, Vermillion hue	I	SO-ST	B
YELLOW-ORANGE							
PY35 HK	Cadmium Yellow		Bright, light, greenish to reddish yellow	Aurora Yellow, Brilliant Yellow, Cad. Yellow from yellow to red bias	I	O-SO	B/D
PY37	Cadmium Yellow		Bright lemon to med to deep reddish yellow	Cadmium Yellow Light, Medium and Deep, Cadmium Yellow Lemon	I	O	B
PY41 N	Naples Yellow		Shades of pale to bright, greenish to red yellow	Antimony Yellow; Genuine Naples Yellow Light, Lead Antimoniate	I	O	C
PY42 LK	Yellow Iron Oxide		Dull Reddish yellow to yellowish orange brown	Golden Ochre, Light Brown, Mars Orange, Mars Yellow, Yellow Ochre	I	O-T	A
PY43 LK	Natural Yellow Iron Oxide		Dull Reddish yellow to yellowish orange brown	Golden Ochre, Raw Sienna, Yellow Ochre	I	SO-T	A
PY65 HK	Hansa Yellow 65		Bright, light, highly saturated, dp red/yellow	Arylide Yellow, Cad. Y hue, Gamboge, Hansa Yellow, Indian Yellow hue	I	SO	A
PY83 LK	Diarylide Yellow HR83		Light, deep yellow, reddish undertone	Azo Yellow, Scheveningen Yellow Deep, Indian Yellow	I	O-ST	A
PY110 LK	Isoindolinone Yellow		Light, deep yellow with red undertone	Gamboge hue, Indian Yellow Orange Extra, Perm. Yellow Deep	I	O	A
PY153	Nickel Dioxime Yellow		Deep yellow. orange to brown undertone	Indian Yellow hue, New Gamboge	I	O-SO	B
YELLOW							
PY3 HK	Hansa Yellow 10G		Bright Lemon yellow with green undertones.	Arylide Yellow, Azo Yellow Lemon, Hansa Yellow, Lemon or Perm. Yellow	II - III	ST-SO	A
PY35	Cadmium Yellow		Bright, light, greenish to reddish yellow	Brilliant Yellow, Cadmium Lemon, Cadmium Yellow, Cad. Lemon Yellow	I	O-SO	B/D

Color Index Number	Color Index Name	Swatch	Color Description	Alternative Names	Permanence	Transparent Opaque	Toxicity
			YELLOW				
PY40 LK	Aureoline		Med to dull golden yellow Mustard yellow)	Aureolin, Cobalt Yellow, Yellow Lake, Cobalt Yellow Lake	I - II	ST-T	C
PY53 HK	Nickel Antimony Titanium Yellow		Pale, light greenish lemon yellow	Nickel Titante Yellow, Titanium Yellow	I	O-ST	A
PY74	Arylide Yellow 5GX		Mid to greenish yellow w/cool to warm hues.	Arylide, Azo Yellow, Cad. Yellow hue, Hansa, Monoazo Yellow, Perm. Yellow	I - II	SO-ST	A
PY150 LK	Nickel Azo Yellow	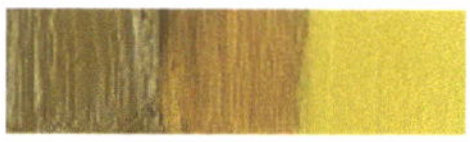	Deep dull reddish yellow	Aureoline, Indian Yellow hue, Nickel Azo, Transparent Golden Yellow	I	ST	B
PY154	Benzimidazolone Yellow		Bright, light greenish through to mid yellow	Azo, Benzimidazolone Yellow, Primary Yellow, Pure Yellow, Transparent Yellow	I-II	ST	A
PY175 HK	Benzimidazolone Yellow H6G		Bright light lemon yellow, green undertone	Chrome Yellow Lemon, Lemon Yellow Hue, Permanent Yellow Lemon	I	ST	A
			YELLOW-GREEN				
PY3 & PG7 or PG36	Mixes of Hansa 10G, Phthalo Green.		Yellow green	Cinnabar Green Extra Light, Permanent Green Light, Yellow Green	I-III	ST	A
PY154 & PG7	Benzimidazolone Yellow Green	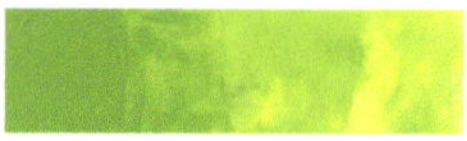	Yellow green	Permanent Yellowish Green, Van Gogh watercolor	I	SO-ST	A
PG7 & PY154 HK	Phthalo Green and Benzimidazolone	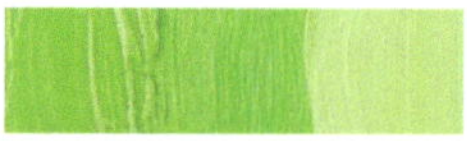	Yellow green	Permanent Yellow Green, Rembrandt oil	I	ST-T	A
PG10	Nickel Azo Yellow		Greenish Yellow	Gold Bronze; Indian Yellow Substitute; Nickel Azo			
PY129 LK	Irgazin Yellow		Slightly dull, light yellowish green	Azo Green, Green Gold, Golden Green	I	T	C
PY138 LK	Quinophthalone Yellow	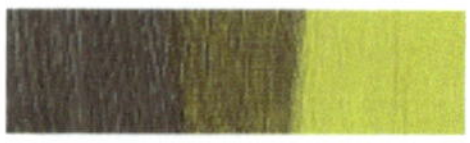	Very light, bright, green to reddish yellow	Permanent Lemon Yellow, Pigment Yellow, Quinopthalone Yellow	I	O-ST	A
			GREEN				
PG7	Phthalocyanine Green (blue shade)		Deep Green Blue	Phthalo Green, Rembrandt Green, Scheveningen Green Deep	I	T	A
PG17 LK	Chrome Oxide Green	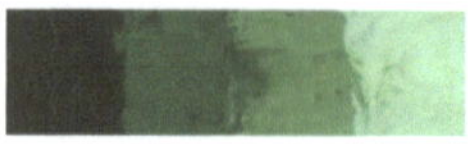	Dullish yellowish green to mid Green	Chrome Oxide, Chromium Oxide Green, Oxide Chromium	I*	O	A
PG18	Viridian		Dull mid green to bluish green	Emerald Green, Oxyde Verte, Permanent Green, Viridian Green Deep	I	T	A
PG19 HK	Cobalt Green	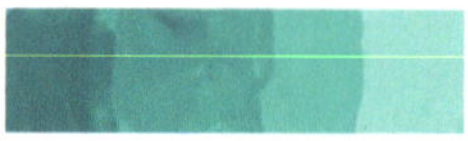	Dull yellowish to bluish green	Cobalt Green, Cobalt Green Turquoise, Oriental Green	I	O	B

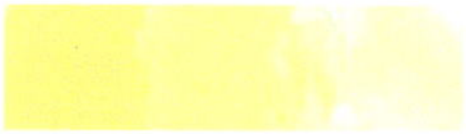

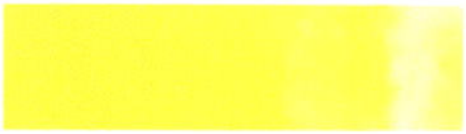

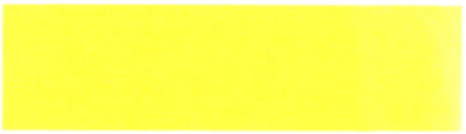

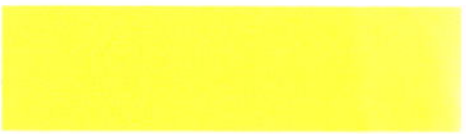

Color Index Number	Color Index Name	Swatch	Color Description	Alternative Names	Permanence	Transparent Opaque	Toxicity
GREEN							
PG23 LK	Green Earth		Dull, bluish to light yellow greens	Celadon Green, Green Earth, Terre Verte	I	SO-T	A
PG26 LK	Cobalt Chromite Green		Dull bluish green	Camouflage Green; Cobalt Chromite, Coblat Green	I*	ST	B
PG36	Phthalocyanine Green (yellow shade)		Green to yellowish green	Cyan Grn., Emerald, Light Green, Perm. Green, Phthalo or Thalo Green	I	T	A
PG50 HK	Cobalt Titanate Green		Dull Olive green to bright mid green	Cobalt Green, Cobalt Teal, Cobalt Turquoise, Light Green Oxide	I	SO	B
BLUE-GREEN							
PB15 or PB 15:1	Phthalocyanine Blue RS		Intense deep blue in reddish bright blue tones	Cerulean Blue Hue, Phthalo Blue RS	I	T	A
PB 15:3	Phthalocyanine Blue (green shade)		Intense deep blue green	Cyan Blue, Cobalt Blue, Cerulean Blue, Manganese Blue, Monestial Blue, Phthalo	I	T	A
PB16	Heliogen Blue L7560		Intense deep green blue in mass tone	Caribbean Blue, Heliogen Blue, Helio, Turquoise Green, Phthalo Blue Green	I	T	A
PB17	Phthalocyanine Cyan		Bright greenish blue	Antique Turquoise, Peacock Blue, Phthalocyanine Cyan, Pure Blue	I	T	A
PB27 LK	Prussian Blue		Deep dark blue, green undertone	Iron Blue, Milori Blue, Paris Blue, Parisian (Prussian), Blue Extra	I - II	T	C
PB35 HK	Cerulean Blue		Light greenish blue	Cerulean Blue, Cerulean Blue Genuine, Cobalt Blue Green, Coeruleum	I	SO	B
BLUE							
PB36 HK	Cobalt Chromite		Light greenish blue	Aquamarine, Cerulean Blue, Colbalt Turquoise, Teal Green, Topaz Blue	I	SO	B
PB28 HK	Cobalt Blue		Greenish to mid-shade blue	Cerulean Blue hue, Cobalt Blue, Kings Bl., Primary Bl., Royal Bl., Smalt Blue	I	ST	B
PB60 LK	Indanthrone Blue		Dark reddish blue	Anthraquinone, Indanthrene Blue, Delft Blue, Indigo, Royal Blue	I	T	B
PB74	Cobalt Zinc Silicate Blue		Deep or dark mid-shade to reddish blue	Cobalt Blue Deep, Sapphire Blue	I	ST-T	B
BLUE-VIOLET							
PB29 HK	Ultramarine Blue		Deep blue, violet	Azurite, French Ultramarine Blue, Lapis Lazuli, Perm. Blue, Ultramarine Blue	I	T	A
PB60 LK	Indanthrene Blue		Dark reddish blue	Anthraquinone, Indanthrone Blue, Delft Blue, Royal Blue	I	T	B

Color Index Number	Color Index Name	Swatch	Color Description	Alternative Names	Permanence	Transparent Opaque	Toxicity
BLUE-VIOLET							
PB66 LK	Indigo		Deep dark blue pigment, almost violet	Indigo	I - III	ST-T	A
VIOLET							
PV14 HK	Cobalt Violet		Light reddish to deep dark blue violet	Cobalt Magenta, Cobalt Rose, Cobalt Violet Dark	I	SO-ST	C
PV15	Ultramarine Violet		Blue shade to mid-shade	Mineral Violet, Ultramarine Blue French, Ultramarine Red, Ultramarine Violet	I	ST	A
PV16	Manganese Violet		Red shade to blue shade deep purple	Manganese Violet, Permanent Blue Violet	I	SO	C
PV19	Quinacridone Violet		Bright to deep bluish to reddish violet	Magenta, Permanent Magenta, Quinacridone Alizarin Crimson or Red	I	T	B
PV23	Dioxazine Violet		Deep dark blue or red shade violet	Blue Violet, Deep, Violet; Dioxazine Purple, Dioxazine Mauve, Permanent Violet	I - II	O-ST	A
PV29	Perylene Violet		Dark dull red purple	Anthraquinone Violet, Perylene Violet	I	T	A
PV37	Dioxazine Violet		Red and blue shades of dark deep purple	Dioxazine Purple, Permanent Violet. Note: PV37 is more lightfast than PV23	I - II	ST	B
PV42	Quinacridone Violet/Maroon		Dull reddish violet	Magenta, Quinacridone Pink, Royal Purple Lake	I	ST	A
PV47 HK	Cobalt Lithium Violet Phosphate		Red shade violet	Cobalt Violet, HO	I	-	B
PR101 LK	Synthetic Iron Oxide Red		Brownish yellow, orange, or red w/violet tones	Caput Mortuum, Mars Violet, Red Oxide	I	O-T	A
RED-VIOLET							
PR83	Alizarin Crimson		Deep Dark Bordeaux with a maroon mass tone	Alizarin Crimson, Carmine Alizarin Crimson, Rose Madder. Note: this is NOT a recommended color.	III-IV	T	A
PR122	Quinacridone Red		Clean bright blue shade light red	Acra Red, Alizarin, Crimson Lake, Perm. Alizarin Crimson, Quinacridone	I	SO-T	B
PR177	Anthraquinone Red		Blue shade deep red	Burgundy Wine, Crimson Lake, Perm. Alizarin Crimson, Rose Madder	I - II	T	B
PR175 LK	Benzimidazolone Red		Dull, yellowish red	Benzimidazolone Maroon	I	O	A
PR179 LK	Pereylene Maroon		Deep violet red	Florentine Red SH, Pereylene Maroon	I	T	A

Color Index Number	Color Index Name	Swatch	Color Description	Alternative Names	Permanence	Transparent Opaque	Toxicity
			RED-VIOLET				
PR209 HK	Quinacridone Red		Pinkish to mid red	Crimson Lake, Madder Lake, Perm. Red, Quinacridone Red, Ruby Lake	I	T	A
PR221 HK	Pigment Red 221		Bluish red	Carmine, Pink Madder, Rose Madder	II	T	A
PR264 HK	Pyrrole Red Rubine		Dark deep red, violet undertone	Crimson Lake, Perm. Alizarin Crimson, Permanent Madder, Pyrrole Crimson	I - II	ST	A
			WHITE				
PW1	Lead White		Warm	Cremnitz, Flake White, Lead White. *Note: Most manufacturers have stopped production.*	I	O	D
PW4	Zinc Oxide White		Zinc Buff Yellowish light pale yellow	Chinese White, Zinc White	I	T-ST	B
PW6	Titanium White		Purest White	Permanent White, Titanium White.	I	O	A
BLACK							
PBk6	Carbon Black		Black with Brown, Blue or Neutral Undertone	Blue Black, Lamp Black	I	SO	A
PBk7	Lamp Black		Deep Black, brown undertone	Carbon Black, Ivory Black	I	O	A
PBk8	Vine Black		Undertone can be bluish to brownish	Carbon Black, Charcoal Black, Vine Black	II	SO	A
PBk9	Bone Black		Brownish Black	Ivory Black, Lamp Black	I	SO	B
PBk11	Mars Black		Bluish gray to black	Iron Black; Iron Oxide, Mars Black	I	SO	A
PBk28	Mineral Black		Bluish black to jet black	Jet Black, Ebony Black, Neutral Black, Copper Chromite Black.	I	O	B
BROWN							
PBr6 N	Iron Oxide Hydroxide Brown		Exist in shades from yellow thru violet	Brown Iron Oxide, Brown Ochre Goethite, Dutch Brown	I	O	A
PBr7 N	Iron Oxides		Exist in shades from yellow thru violet	Brown Ochre, Burnt Umber, Raw Sienna, Raw Umber, Red Oxide, Van Dyke Brown	I	O	A
PBr24 N	Chrome Antimony Titanate		Light yellowish to reddish brown to golden orange	Naples Yellow, Yellow Ochre Light	I	O	A

LEGEND
Permanence: I = Excellent, II = Good, III = Poor, IV = Fugitive, extremely poor
Transparency: O = Opaque, SO = Semi-Opaques, ST = Semi-Transparent, T = Transparent
Toxicity: A = Low Hazard, B = Possible hazard if handled improperly, C = Hazardous, use precaution when handling,
D = Extremely Toxic. Letters following CI #: HK = High Key color, LK = Low Key color, N = Neutral

Glossary of Terms

Achromatic – Without color, a colorless scheme using black, white, and gray.

Analogous – Using any shades, tints or tones of colors that lie next to each other on the wheel.

Analogous Complementary – Is made up of a pair of Complementary colors plus two to four added colors either side of one of the Complementary colors.

Chroma – The strength, brightness, or purity of a color, is its chroma (or intensity)

Color Scheme – A choice of colors assembled in a systematic order to create a harmonious painting. Triad, Tetrad or Complementary are among the many types of color schemes.

Complementary Color – *Making something else or making it better* as in the complementary colors. These are two hues directly opposite one another on the Color Wheel. The Complement to RED is GREEN, the complement to YELLOW is VIOLET and the complement to BLUE is ORANGE. Combine a color with its complementary to produce neutral colors such as browns and earth tones found in nature.

Complimentary - *Flattering or given free as a courtesy*. This spelling is often confused with the definition of complementary which is used when referring to colors opposite on the Color Wheel.

Cool Colors – Colors whose visual temperature makes them seem cool are YELLOW-GREEN, GREEN, BLUE-GREEN, BLUE, BLUE-VIOLET and VIOLET. Cool colors often make objects appear to recede. RED-ORANGE may also be referred to as a cool color when used to describe the temperature in relationship to ORANGE.

Earth Colors - Pigments such as Yellow Ochre, Burnt Sienna and Raw and Burnt Umber, are obtained by mining. They are usually compounds of metals.

Glaze – To form a thin transparent layer on top of another to create a new hue.

Gray – A hue that is void of any color spectrum pigments. It is derived by mixing white and black.

Harmonious Color - Established when a color scheme such as a Triad, Tetrad or a Complementary are used.

High Intensity (or High Key) – Use of predominately pale, light, or bright values used on the overall painting.

Hue – The term used to name a color of the spectrum, i.e. red, yellow, and blue. Another word for color.

Intensity – The strength, brightness, or purity of a color, is its intensity or chroma.

Juxtaposition - When colors are placed next to each other, the intensity and effect may produce interactions of harmony or conflict.

Limited Palette – Refers to the use of colors selected in a harmonious color scheme and not using a full spectrum of colors.

Local Color – Refers to the actual color of an object.

Low Intensity (or Low Key) – Consistent use of dull, dark color values on the overall painting.

Middle Key – Using a full value scale, brightening sun-bleached areas to near white, and intensifying the shadows to very dark.

Monochrome – Using one color with the addition of white and/or black to create varying shades, tints, or tones of that color.

Neutral Color – Neutral colors are found in tube colors with names like Paynes Gray and Neutral Tint. A neutral color can be mixed using two complementary colors.

Opaque Color – Impenetrable by light. Not transparent or translucent.

Primary Colors – Colors that cannot be mixed from any other colors; RED, YELLOW, and BLUE. From these primaries, most all other colors can be mixed.

Saturation – The purity or intensity of a color (hue) on a scale from bright (full saturation) to dull (low saturation), as measured by the intensity of the hue undiluted with white. Also referred to as chroma.

Secondary Colors – The resulting hues of mixing two primaries i.e. RED plus YELLOW = ORANGE, YELLOW plus BLUE = GREEN and BLUE plus RED = VIOLET.

Shade – A color with black added.

Spectral Colors – Colors that can be produced by a narrow band of wavelengths of visible light (monochromatic light) are called pure spectral colors. The various color ranges of the spectrum are continuous, with no clear boundaries between one color and the next.

Split Complementary – A Color Scheme using the color on each side of its complement on the Color Wheel.

Split Primary – A Color Scheme using a warm and a cool of each primary color.

Tertiary Colors – Tertiary colors are combined names of the adjacent primary and secondary colors therefore having a double word name. These colors make up half of the twelve color groups on the Color Wheel. These colors are RED-VIOLET, RED-ORANGE, YELLOW-ORANGE, YELLOW-GREEN, BLUE-GREEN and BLUE-VIOLET

Tetrad – A contrast of four colors on the Color Wheel which equates to two sets of complementary colors.

Tint – A color with white or water added as in watercolor.

Tone – When gray is added to a color it is considered a tone.

Translucent Color – A Semi-Transparent color between Transparent and Semi-Opaque. Allows light to pass through but not enough to see detail through it. Diffused light.

Transparent Color – A color which is thin in pigment when applied to paper or canvas. Transparent colors allow the under color (or white of paper or canvas) to show through.

Triad – A Color Scheme in which three colors are equally spaced from each other on the Color Wheel i.e. 3 primary colors – RED, YELLOW, and BLUE form a Triad.

Value – Light and dark qualities of a surface or area sometimes referred to as tonal values.

Warm Color – Colors whose visual temperature makes them seem warm. These colors are RED-VIOLET, RED, RED-ORANGE, ORANGE, YELLOW- ORANGE and YELLOW. Warm colors often make objects appear to come forward. BLUE-VIOLET may also be referred to as a warm color when used to describe the temperature in relationship to BLUE.

About the Author

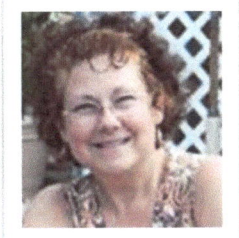

Born into a family of musicians, Elaine began her own artistic journey at an early age. She studied art worldwide through classes and workshops with renowned artists. Landscapes have always been her love, where shapes, textures and lighting always offer an endless source of subjects and challenges.

She has a deep connection to the natural world around her and enjoys taking part in translating natures' inspirations to canvas. Her current body of work focuses on the New England landscape with emphasis on historical settings throughout the New England area. She holds the Hudson River Valley Artists in high regard for their valuable studies en plein air along with their classical academic approach to painting. She strives to remain faithful to this process when creating her own art by experiencing the mood of the landscape en plein air and walking off the beaten path to create a small drawing or painting studies, usually for use on larger studio pieces.

Elaine has been a professional artist since 1985, began teaching in 1991 and continues to offer fine art classes and workshops. Through her teaching experiences her students led her to focus on developing this easy to understand, color mixing approach, for use by working artists, teachers, and the novice painter.

A national award-winning artist, Elaine is an active art exhibit participant in juried shows, has several images licensed for commercial use. She also prides herself as an active advocate of the fine arts in her community.

Connect with Elaine

Elaine Farmer Website - Workshop Schedule, printable practice Color Wheels and Inventory Sheets can be found at www.WhiteBirchFineArt.com under Classes.

Can't travel to NH for a workshop? Schedule one for your group in your town!

Paperback & Kindle - Amazon.com

Facebook - https://www.facebook.com/WhiteBirchFineArt

Instagram - https://Instagram.com/ElaineFarmerArt

YouTube - https://www.youtube.com/@elaineart56

e-book version - Smashwords.com

Acknowledgement

Thank you to The Color Wheel Company for the permission to allow me to illustrate the use of their impertinent tool, *The Color Wheel*, throughout the book.

Contributors

Image and Photo Credits

The Color Wheel Company
Image Tec Photo Tom Grassi, Photographer of Elaine B Farmer images
Dachowski Photography Photographer of Elaine B Farmer images
Drew Caron, Videographer and Editor for e-book version

Editors

Sharon Allen, Derry, NH
Leslie Toomy, Londonderry, NH

Selected Bibliography

Carlson, John F., N.A.; Carlson's Guide to Landscape Painting
Leland, Nita; Confident Color
Zhang, Hongnian and Woolley; Lois; The Yin/Yang of Painting

Website References

American Society of Testing Materials - http://www.astm.org/ABOUT/factsheet.html

Pigment identification - http://www.artiscreation.com/Color_index_names.html

Van Gogh article on browning of his Yellows –

http://www.stltoday.com/news/science/article_cf84d524-38c4-11e0-843a-00127992bc8b.html

INDEX

1

www.ingramcontent.com/pod-product-compliance
Lightning Source LLC
Chambersburg PA
CBHW050720180526
45159CB00003B/1081